ALL
OUR
LOSSES,
ALL
OUR
GRIEFS

Book by Kenneth R. Mitchell and Herbert Anderson
Published by The Westminster Press
All Our Losses, All Our Griefs: Resources for Pastoral Care

Books by Kenneth R. Mitchell
*Psychological and Theological Relationships in the Multiple
    Staff Ministry*
Hospital Chaplain

ALL OUR LOSSES, ALL OUR GRIEFS

RESOURCES FOR PASTORAL CARE

Kenneth R. Mitchell
and
Herbert Anderson

THE WESTMINSTER PRESS
Philadelphia

BOOK DESIGN BY ALICE DERR

Published by The Westminster Press®
Philadelphia, Pennsylvania

PRINTED IN THE UNITED STATES OF AMERICA
9 8 7 6 5

Library of Congress Cataloging in Publication Data

Mitchell, Kenneth R.
All our losses, all our griefs.

Includes bibliographical references and index.
1. Grief. 2. Pastoral theology. I. Anderson,
Herbert, 1936–   . II. Title.
BJ1487.M57 1983   253   83-19851
ISBN 0-664-24493-9 (pbk.)

In Remembrance
of

Ernest Reece Mitchell
June 7, 1897–July 3, 1977

and

Clara Ellen Anderson
August 15, 1906–January 21, 1983

who in different ways taught us
about the costliness of
commitment
and
whose deaths marked out
the beginning and the end
of writing this book

Requiem aeternam dona eis, amen.

Contents

Foreword

This is a book about loss: how serious personal losses take place, why we react to loss as we do, how many important forms of loss go unnoticed, how we can recover from the impact of loss, and how we can help others to recover from loss. So far as we know, no other approach to the subject of grief has made use of resources similar to ours; furthermore, we have emphasized elements of loss in situations that do not at first appear to be situations of loss and grief. What we have tried to accomplish in the following pages consists of several elements.

First, our resources. For years, both of us have been collecting statements about loss and grief from a wide variety of persons: our friends, our parishioners, our students. By the time we agreed to collaborate on this book, we had amassed records of more than a thousand experiences of loss. We sifted through those records, allowing those with whom we worked to become our teachers. What we have written here comes largely from them. Some of our material is theoretical, but this book essentially comes from the losses and griefs of those who have trusted us with their experiences.

Second, it is our conviction that grief is a normal response to significant loss: grieving is not, as some writers have suggested, evidence of sickness or disease. It is something to live through rather than to cure. It is no more pathological than the rush of adrenalin experienced when one has narrowly escaped danger. Grief is a normal response. It is a disservice to grieving persons to interpret their feelings and behavior as though there were a warp in their psychological makeup, or a deficiency in their spiritual formation.

Third, we are convinced that many people, including such potential helpers as Christian pastors, are unaware of the many kinds of loss that are an ordinary part of life. Grief is usually thought of as a response to the death of a loved one. That is, to be sure, the most profound and personal form that loss takes for most people. Powerful as the death of a loved one is, it is not death that teaches us what loss and grief are. We learn about loss much earlier in life; it comes, in fact, before we know much about death at all. Death is only one form of loss. Our purpose is to help caring persons become more sensitive to the many instances in life when a "grief ministry" is called for. We have intended to be thorough in our attention to this aspect, considering not only such losses as death and divorce, but also less easily noticeable experiences that involve significant loss.

Fourth, we also intend this book to be squarely within the discipline of pastoral theology. There are several books on funerals and on ministering to the bereaved which are good indicators of "what to do." There are other good books designed to help grief sufferers work their way through the grieving process. As pastoral theologians, we have drawn upon the resources both of theology and of the human sciences to guide both private and public ministries with those who grieve. We have included in one volume three questions that have often been dealt with separately: (1) Why do people grieve, or what is the genesis of grief in human life? (2) What are the dynamics of grief and the characteristics of grieving? (3) How can we help those who grieve? That scope is part of the uniqueness of this book.

Although our original intention was to produce a source for the teaching of pastoral care in seminaries, we have also written this book as a resource for all persons who care about others suffering from loss and grief. We believe that pastoral work with mourners is the work of the congregation, not just of certain professionals. Thus, this book is intended for any person who wants to understand loss and grief, whether to minister to others or to come to terms with one's own experience.

PART 1

THE GENESIS
OF GRIEF

1
The Pervasiveness
of Loss and Grief

Experiences that evoke grief are both more frequent and more varied than most people imagine. The death of a person one loves is such an obvious occasion of grief that many people have come to think of it as the only such occasion. The result of that misunderstanding is that many people have experienced lengthened suffering from unrecognized grief.

Our first task in this book is to explore the genesis of grief: to understand what can cause grief and how that cause has its roots in childhood experience. We begin the exploration with several vignettes, each a tale of grief triggered by a significant loss, but none having to do directly with the death of a loved person.

VIGNETTES OF LOSS AND GRIEF

1. BILL WEATHERBY'S HOMETOWN

Bill Weatherby had lived in Springfield for his first eighteen years. He left for college, joined the Army, and now in his early forties, was coming home again. He looked forward to seeing familiar places and people.

However, his favorite fishing creek was filled with foul-smelling waste. The butcher shop where Bill had shopped was now a saloon. Main Street was a cross-country high-way. His own "big, white house on a high hill" was now a dark gray with bright-blue trim, and it stood on a slight rise.

Bill remembered that his old high school classmate Roy Jenkins had bought the Texaco station on the west side of town. He drove out to the station and there was Roy, grayer but otherwise looking pretty much the same as Bill had remembered him. "Hello, Roy!" said Bill, and Roy replied: "Do I know you?" Bill introduced himself, and there was a pleasant enough conversation, but Roy's "Do I know you?" rattled around in Bill's mind for days after-ward. One night Bill dreamed of a parade of old friends marching past him, each one asking "Do I know you?" In the background of the dream stood a large white house on a high hill.

2. JACK MURTAGH'S DEPRESSION

By the time he was forty-two, Jack Murtagh was the head of the Oklahoma City branch of a large corporation, and widely respected throughout the company. He under-stood both production and sales, and represented the company well in the community. On the basis of his success and skill, the company promoted Jack, made him their chief legislative liaison, and moved him and his family to Washington.

Jack did not deceive himself; he knew that his title was a fancy term meaning lobbyist. He was excited by the change at first, but it did not take long for disillusionment to set in. In Oklahoma City he had had a strong say in influencing company policy, and had run his division as he saw fit. Now he was merely a mouthpiece for policies he had no hand in devising, and with which he often bitterly disagreed. He hated living in Washington; compared to Oklahoma City he found it phony.

As soon as he reasonably could, Jack sought and received a transfer to Omaha. But gradually he realized that part of what made life worthwhile for him was having "real responsibility"; it was clear that he would never again have that. He had been sidetracked. It was almost impossible for him to drag himself to work.

Mandy Murtagh insisted that they seek the pastor's help, believing that their marriage was deteriorating. The pastor heard the story, and realized that Jack was depressed. When he suggested to Mandy and Jack that perhaps Jack was grieving, Jack's face lighted up in sudden understanding. Soon after that, Jack took early retirement and went into business for himself. The depression and marital friction disappeared. He said later that taking charge of his own life again required that he develop a new image of himself. The old picture he had had of himself had died.

3. THE MOVING OF FIRST PRESBYTERIAN CHURCH

First Presbyterian Church occupied a distinguished location on the town square across from the courthouse. But one day the town council exercised the right of eminent domain and took the property. The church had to move. The town square would not be the same. The church was architecturally unusual; in particular, the woodwork in the sanctuary was of a unique design.

When the session found a desirable site, architects were invited to submit drawings for a new church. But none of the architects' sketches or proposals was acceptable. No one knew exactly why, but the church was unable to make a decision to employ one of the architects.

The pastor solved the problem. All the architects' plans had called for a chapel. The pastor suggested that the architects change the design of the chapel so that it would resemble as closely as possible the unique appearance of the old sanctuary. Within three days after the new sketches came in, the church settled on a design and was ready to proceed with the next steps. At the suggestion of a contractor, about a third of the woodwork in the old sanctuary was used for the chapel in the new church, and two of the five stained-glass windows from the old church were placed in the new building. Most of the congregation was enthusiastic about the new church as a whole, but it was the new chapel with its old wood and windows to which they proudly took visitors.

THE MANY FORMS OF LOSS AND GRIEF

Two fourteen-year-old girls, best friends since nursery school, are separated when one family moves to California. A popular high school math teacher begins to lose his hearing, and students notice that he is becoming cranky. A key figure in an organization loses his voice when his cancerous larynx is removed, and until he learns to speak again, the organization is paralyzed.

There is a common thread running through all these stories. They are all instances of loss and grief. To say that involves *no trivialization* of grief and the grieving process. It is neither necessary nor wise to limit the terms *grief* and *grieving* to the emotional state and the work that the death of a loved one makes necessary. Nor is it useful to distinguish between losses that evoke grief with a big *G* and grief with a small *g*.[1] Unless we understand that all losses, even "minor" ones, give rise to grief, we shall misunderstand its fundamental nature.

We have already suggested that grief is a normal emotional response to significant loss. The abnormality of grief is frequently a consequence of the refusal to grieve or the inability of the grieving person to find those who are willing to care. Grief is universal and inescapable even when its existence and impact are denied. It is a composite of powerful emotions assailing us whenever we lose someone or something we value. Grieving is the intentional work grief-stricken persons engage in, enabling them to return eventually to full, satisfying lives. It can be avoided, though at a very high cost to the one who refuses it. We must identify some aspects of the formation of personality in the early years of life, what infants and children experience as loss, and how they experience it in order to understand the genesis of grief in life. Loss, not death, is the normative metaphor for understanding those experiences in human life that produce grief.

2
Attachment, Separation, and Grief

We begin life connected. An unborn baby is joined to a mother who provides the nutrients and environment necessary for the development of a new life. The relationship of the fetus to the mother is one of utter dependence, a matter of sheer survival. Every human being begins life's sojourn the same way.

The pregnancy ends; the uterine attachment is broken; the child is born. The first experience of separation for every human being is birth. Some writers argue that the turbulent experience of being expelled from the womb is the origin of all emotional disturbance.[2] Such a birth trauma may not be the root of all emotional problems, but it is true that being born is our first experience of separation. Being thrust from the safety of the womb is likely to be a shock; but it is also necessary for independent life. Just as the connection between mother and child is necessary for survival before birth, so the separation *at* birth is necessary for the beginning of distinct human life.

This brings us to a fundamental thesis: *The genesis of grief lies in the inevitability of both attachment and separation for the sustenance and development of human life.* The biological connection necessary for the survival of the fetus prior to birth continues in social forms throughout life. At the same time, the development of the person as a distinct human

being requires separation: first from the mother biological-
ly, then from mother and others psychologically. Being
born is the beginning of autonomous life, but it is also an
experience of loss. Just as there can be no life without
attachment, there can be no attachments without eventual
separation and loss. Grief has its beginnings in the twin
necessities of attachment and separation. There is no life
without either attachment or loss; hence there is no life
without grief. To become a separate individual involves
undergoing a first lesson in mortality.[3]

THREE APPROACHES
TO ATTACHMENT AND SEPARATION

Three similar but distinct ways of thinking about attachment and separation have informed our thinking. Each
casts a slightly different light on the experience of grief.

Margaret Mahler's studies of the *mother-child relationship*
help us to understand several powerful emotions—particularly anxiety about one's own survival—that accompany
loss. Melanie Klein and others have developed a theory of
object relations, which helps to clarify how human beings
invest themselves in other things and persons, and why
most changes in life carry with them a powerful element of
loss. John Bowlby has written extensively about the process of *attachment*, which helps us to understand how the
problems of attachment and separation from childhood
continue throughout adult life.

1. Margaret Mahler: Severing Symbiosis

Before an infant is born, its relationship to the mother is
one of complete connectedness and dependence. Margaret
Mahler has borrowed the term *symbiosis* from biology to
describe this relationship.[4] Birth severs this biological
symbiosis. For the first few months after birth, the infant
continues to be dependent on others to "supply and

deliver raw materials free." The dependency is absolute; the infant can do nothing for itself except give off cries which may serve as signals. Nurture, mobility, protection, warmth: all these things, and indeed life itself, are provided by others.

Mahler has labeled this psychological and social continuation of the original biological connection between mother and child "social symbiosis." She writes: "The intrauterine, parasite-host relationship within the mother is enveloped, as it were, in the extrauterine matrix of the mother's nursing care, a kind of social symbiosis."[5] All the infant's early experiences tend to reinforce this impression that the infant is its own whole world. The warmth of mother's body and the food coming from her seem available merely for the wishing. The things that from an adult perspective are externals are experienced by the baby as portions of the self; and nothing really exists but the self.

Infants are, from an adult point of view, totally selfish; they have no way of acknowledging or even of recognizing a boundary between self and not-self. But this selfishness evokes no moral disapproval from any sensible adult; it is accepted because the infant knows no other life as yet. This will be important to remember in any study of grief. The experience of loss at any time in life triggers a momentary preoccupation with self that is necessary for psychological survival, just as the infant's preoccupation with self is vital to its biological survival. At a moment of significant loss, needs for sustenance and protection mount sharply and are often left unsatisfied; at such a point the grief-stricken person may recapitulate that early infant selfishness to the point that others notice and perhaps even condemn it.

At about the age of three months, the baby begins to see things differently. The process of separation starts. Mahler calls this "psychological birth" or "hatching," the process by which the infant moves toward becoming a separate, distinct self. It can happen simply: the child cries and mother does not come; or, if mother comes, she does not do what is expected. If nurturers have provided reasonable stability for the child, the experience may be relatively smooth. But if security is lacking, the infant experiences a disturbance in its fragile, evolving self.

This psychological birth, or hatching, requires a restructuring of one's entire world, and is inevitably accompanied by loss and grief. Mahler suggests that the emotional response to such breaking and remaking of a world is not protest, but diminished activity and a low-keyed emotional tone resembling withdrawal. The process of becoming a separate self is painful, though we value the results. This experience of separation, essential for the formation of the self, is also the fundamental experience of loss to which all subsequent experiences of loss throughout life will be referred. It is not surprising, then, that we should find patterns of selfishness and withdrawal in grief whenever it occurs.

2. Melanie Klein: Outside Objects Inside Me

At first, the distinction between "self" and "other" is simple. The infant begins to be able to distinguish between me and not-me. This in turn makes attachment to others possible. Then the infant begins to divide the "other" into distinguishable objects: mother, father, other persons, physical objects. In object relations theory, all these persons and things are referred to as *objects*. The infant, having learned to make a distinction between self and object, demands a firm attachment to the object: "It may not be *me*, but it is *mine*."

Next, as the infant gradually relinquishes its hold on the actual object—mother, sister, food—it begins to build an internal mental image of the object, so that when the actual object is not present, the child has the image to hold on to. In object relations theory this mental image is called an "internal construct." For this internal construct to be an accurate representation of the object, the object itself must first be present with relative consistency and frequency. The child maintains relationships with these internal constructs, just as she or he would with the actual external object. The development of a lively sense of self depends on having an internal world of reliable images to which one is attached.[6]

As the child begins to separate and move away, it is important that the mother or another nurturing person remain available on a consistent basis. If that does not happen, the result is called premature object loss. Not only does this lead to a distorted mental image of the lost object; it also evokes a sense of disorganization and even dissolution of the self. The development, in human beings, of an autonomous self requires the presence of dependable objects, the capacity to make emotional connections *and* the ability to cope with some object loss.

Object relations theory goes well beyond the concepts of Sigmund Freud. Freud did recognize the existence of powerful attachments, significant emotional investments in something or someone outside oneself, and labeled such attachments *Besetzungen*, "occupations," in the sense of occupying territory. (English translations have for some reason used a Greek word, *kathexis*, to translate Freud's German here, with a resultant loss of clarity and meaning.) Freud's understanding was that becoming "occupied" by another was primarily a function of instinct, a mechanical satisfaction of needs.

Object relations theory is considerably less mechanistic. According to Melanie Klein, the human psyche is much more than a bundle of instincts. It is a highly personalized world of internalized relationships with significant objects. It may be realistic or distortion-laden, but it is always highly individualized. Each individual internalizes the world in a way unique to that person; therefore, no two experiences of loss are the same, and grief is always personal.[7]

Three important aspects of object relations theory influence our understanding of grief: continuity, ambiguity, and the transitional object.

Continuity

The presence in our minds of a consistent, reliable image of significant figures from the past creates a hedge against a sense of discontinuity. Even when one's internal world contains distorted images, it is generally perceived as continuous with a real past. Our images of the world around us are an important defense against feelings of complete discontinuity.

Ambiguity

What we internalize does not always have a positive value for us. It should not be surprising, then, that grief is always ambiguous. The recognition that the internal world of the self is composed of both "good" and "bad" objects is the second contribution of object relations theory to our understanding of grief. The truth about almost any human relationship is that it has its good and bad aspects; no relationship is 100 percent good or 100 percent bad. But in the very young there is a tendency to see objects as all good or all bad.

This oversimplification lessens as we grow more mature, but never completely disappears. It is often difficult to respond to other people without making them into ideal lovers or sinister persecutors, instead of human beings with limitations and imperfections, with whom it is possible to form a genuine relationship. Therefore, when in either childhood or adulthood someone disappears or ceases to love or dies, those left behind may internalize the lost person as a bad object. This happens to a child when the mother refuses the breast or is punitive or absent; it also happens when the person we need is emotionally detached or unresponsive. The lost object becomes a highly charged internalized "bad" object. We should not be surprised when the loss of a valued object generates feelings of rejection and anger.

> At twenty-four, Carrie had just completed nurses' training, when her grandfather died. The family gathered briefly at the hospital, and then departed, leaving Carrie on the hospital steps with the promise that she would hear later about funeral plans. Eleven years later, she wrote: "The behavior of my mother when her father died rekindled earlier experiences of abandonment. She should never have become a mother. She hated it and hence hated my brother and myself. She would have abandoned us as children if society had allowed her to. When she abandoned me on the day grandfather died, she was enacting what she had wanted to do twenty-four years earlier. This I knew instinctively. The death of my grandfather did not only mean losing someone I would miss, but it meant abandonment, which meant death, my death."

Carrie had internalized her mother as a bad object. Much of her life had been lived in expectation of further abandonment. The intensity and complexity of grief in adult life is often linked to early experiences of object loss. Even necessary separations may be regarded as painful replicas of earlier abandonment. The external world ceases to be a trustworthy place. Carrie became obese in later life in an effort to create protection from further abandonment.

The Transitional Object

For the child, the transitional object softens the terrifying process of separation from mother by providing an object that symbolizes the fusion of the infant and mother in the midst of their separation. The object is usually first offered to the child by the mother; this strengthens the symbolic fusion. The transitional object is not-me, and yet it is so much under my control that I can think of it as part of me. The teddy bear is often cited as the classic example of the transitional object. Or, like Linus in the *Peanuts* comic strip, the child becomes attached to a blanket. The transitional object eases the stress of transition from symbiosis through separation to object constancy and the possibility of attachment.

Transitional objects may also provide a similar function for adults who experience traumatic loss. They help us preserve the mental organization associated with a good object relation that has been lost. In painfully awkward words, a divorced man of thirty-five described how he "hugged a pillow to sleep." Somehow hugging a pillow helped him to endure the pain of loss and sleeping alone. The clothes of a missing person, still hanging in their place in the closet, function as transitional objects to accommodate a painful loss by perpetuating a lingering union with the lost object.

3. JOHN BOWLBY: ATTACHMENT AND SEPARATION

The inevitability of attachment has much to do with grief, and separation is as essential for autonomous life as the earlier attachment is for biological survival. The work of John Bowlby on attachment, separation, and loss draws particular attention to this theme. Bowlby's studies indicate that attachment behavior is primary, autonomous, and lifelong: primary, because the initial bonding to another human being is determined by patterns of imprinting inherent in the higher primates; autonomous, because (as Bowlby points out) the infant's actions influence the response of the primary caretakers; lifelong, because the need for attachment—which is not the same as dependence—continues throughout life.[8] The making and keeping of affectional bonds is an interactional process that is more than either instinct or learned behavior.

Adult attachments are a straightforward continuation of childhood affectional bonds. Adult attachment is not an infantile need that we outgrow or a regression to a state of infantile dependency. The desire to be loved and cared for is fundamental to human nature in adults as well as children. Since our need to love and be loved never ends, the possibility of loss is present throughout life.

Bowlby states: "This picture of attachment behavior as a normal and healthy component of man's instinctive equipment leads us also to regard separation anxiety as the natural and inevitable response whenever an attachment figure is unaccountably missing."[9]

The threat, or the actual occurrence, of loss at any time in human life evokes panic, anxiety, sorrow, and anger in keeping with the intensity of the attachment. Because attachment is lifelong, so is grief.

The inability to respond constructively to loss in later life also has its genesis in the child's experience of separation from the mother figure.

Anyone who has left a young child for any length of time can understand quite well the process Bowlby outlines. Protest is first, predicated on the conviction that tears or temper will be effective in bringing mother back.

When the hope of mother's return fades, there is no more reason to protest. At that point, the child becomes quiet. The child may continue to yearn for mother's return, but the dominant emotion is despair. Eventually, if the separation is protracted enough, the child forgets about the mother, becomes detached and unresponsive even when mother finally returns. Even this detachment can mask a yearning for and anger with the lost person. In one way or another, protest, despair, and detachment are integral to the process of grieving throughout life.

Bowlby's hypothesis is significant because he identifies

the child's experience of loss as mourning. The loss of mother (and sometimes of father) during the early years (at least until age six) gives rise not only to "primary separation anxiety and grief but to processes of mourning in which aggression, the function of which is to achieve reunion, plays a major part."[10] There is thus a connection between an individual's early affectional bonding with parents and his or her later capacity to make affectional bonds. When that initial bonding is not achieved or prematurely aborted, attachment always produces anxiety. The grieving adult's demand for the absent person's return and reproach against him or her for leaving are continuous with the child's protest in the face of loss.

Attachment is distinguishable from dependency. The relationship of the infant and mother is more a relationship of dependency than of attachment. As the child separates from parents and becomes a distinct self, the dependency diminishes and is replaced by attachment. The alternation of attachment and loss is, therefore, a mark of maturity. When either attachment or loss is distorted or prematurely done away with, human life is diminished.

THEOLOGICAL COMMENT

The assertion that grief is a lifelong human experience because of the necessity of attachment and the inevitability of loss is theologically as well as psychologically true. Our attachment to people and things of this world is a continuation of God's love for creation. Despite the efforts of otherworldly forms of piety to limit the experience of grief by setting limits on attachments of any kind, Christianity continues to be the most materialistic of all religions. In his *Letters of Spiritual Counsel*, Martin Luther insists that, though our grief should be moderate, there is nothing disgraceful or unfaithful about natural affection. We are not stones, nor ought we to be. Human attachment belongs to the intention of God for all being.[11] Thus it is a sign of unfaith when people never mourn.

If nothing is of such value that its loss is the occasion of grief, it is not only sad but actually a denial of the Christian doctrine of creation. The capacity to love and be loved is a remaining mark of the "image of God," distorted by sin though it may be. The overwhelming testimony of the Christian tradition celebrates covenant, calls for love, fosters community, encourages reconciliation, and demonstrates affection. To be a follower of Christ is to love life and to value people and things that God has given to us in such a way that losing them brings sadness.

Creation itself is ordered by bonds of affection. The future of generations depends upon attraction and attachment. The human creature imprinted with the stamp of God cannot *not* love. But finitude, too, is human. Life has built-in limits. Our attachment to persons and things is never forever. Some of these signals of finitude are built into the ordinary process of growing up and aging. Friends move away; children die; buildings are torn down; dreams go unfulfilled; communities change. Even when we know that endings are coming, they come as unwelcome surprises.

As Christians, we confess that finitude is good even when we have difficulty seeing that goodness. Death as the ultimate expression of our limitations is not a violation of God's order. Every significant crisis in human development includes some foretaste of mortality. The infant discovers he or she is not the center of the universe; the two-year-old realizes she or he cannot tyrannize the world; the adolescent leaves home. Learning to live with limits is a lifelong task.

Nonetheless, we continue to ask whether finitude is good. Or is it, since it brings with it so much pain, an evil of some sort? Ernest Becker has suggested that we live in terror of finitude from the beginning of life.[12] The process of growing up, Becker insists, involves a masking of fears by the creation of illusions that become character armor to protect us in our vulnerability. Life is spent establishing alliances with heroes and developing character traits that will fend off the terror of death. Finitude is a human problem because we know we are finite.

By contrast, John Hick has suggested that finitude is good. Only when a life is rounded off by death are we able to see it whole. Our finitude is a sign of providence. God, who has given us what we are, has set the limits to our existence; to be human is to be finite, and that is good.[13]

Even so, we are still anxious and angry in the face of human limitations. We do not want to be reminded that someday we shall die. We do not even like to think we are aging. Every loss and separation in life is an intimation of mortality. We protest because we do not like being limited.

We have chosen loss rather than death as a dominant metaphor for this study in order to insist on the ordinariness of loss and the inescapability of finitude. Death, significant though it is, is one form of loss, one about which we know far less than we know about many other losses. None of us has experienced death and returned to tell the tale. What we know about death we only know by analogy. But we have all known loss and separation.

PART II

THE NATURE
OF LOSS
AND GRIEF

3
The Nature
of Loss

For many persons, the loss occasioned by death is the only loss worthy of significant attention; but the losses to which (unlike the death of a loved one) we do not pay intentional heed may have a more profound impact on us in the long run. Early experience of loss dictates to a large extent how we shall experience the death of those whom we love, but it also influences how we experience other losses and plays a large part in the sense of loss attached to the foreknowledge of our own death.

From the personal statements we have gathered about loss from people, we discover that the losses human beings undergo throughout life may be divided into six major types, each with its own specific meanings. People may minimize the impact of one or more types of loss on their lives, and stress others; but all six types of loss deserve recognition and careful discussion.

Since most experiences of loss are a mixture of several types, it is useful to consider each type separately. It is possible that any kind of loss can come to any human being at any point in the life cycle. Yet some losses are particularly associated with particular periods in life. Although it would be misleading to suggest that we experience losses in a particular order, it is true that for many people the first major losses which they consciously recall are material losses.

SIX MAJOR TYPES OF LOSS

1. MATERIAL LOSS

Material loss is the loss of a physical object or of familiar surroundings to which one has an important attachment. Some adults resist recognizing the importance of material loss, as if to take it seriously might mean that one was either too materialistic or too sentimental. Children will much more easily confess how strong their attachment to a particular object is, and how painful its loss. Most human beings have some kind of powerful attachment to a material object, whether it be a family farmhouse or a favorite jacket. If the farmhouse is one day bulldozed to the ground or the jacket given to the Salvation Army, either is a painful loss. If the object is important because of its origin—a gift, say, from someone deeply loved—it has *extrinsic* value. Other objects may have an *intrinsic* value; we have an investment in them for some quality of their own. Objects with extrinsic value attached to another human being whom we love cause the deepest pain when lost.

> In October [writes a student] I lost a pocketknife I'd had for seven and a half years. It was special because an Appalachian mountain man swapped knives with me (a sign of close friendship) and it had more than just a utilitarian purpose. I felt guilty because I had lost a knife a friend had entrusted to me. Over Christmas I replaced that knife with the best quality knife I could find for a moderate amount of money.

Many persons who have undergone material loss report an almost irresistible urge to replace the lost object. In some cases where a comparable replacement is impossible because of the expense, a copy or some other symbolic replacement is substituted. Those who replace lost material objects often conclude that the replacement is never quite the same as the original, even when by objective standards it is better in quality or costs more.

Material loss is frequently, though not universally, the first loss of which the child is consciously aware. Early material losses take familiar forms: the scoop of ice cream that falls from the cone, the toy broken too badly to be mended, the softball confiscated by an angry neighbor. From an adult's point of view, such losses are easily replaced. But if a caring adult fails to take the child's sense of loss seriously, and emphasizes the ease of replacement, the child may construct a fantasy world in which all lost objects can be replaced. This is untrue; and when the child discovers that fact, the sense of loss is compounded.

The fact that some material losses are replaceable may mask the grief reaction accompanying any loss. The grief may show through only in the sense that the replacement is never quite so good as the original.

The loss of a pet is an occasion of grief for adults as well as for children. The intensity of the grief is not surprising. The relationships between people and their pets are charged with quasi-human characteristics, so that we feel that our pets are almost human. And yet grief over the death of a pet has several striking characteristics of material loss. Most people immediately replace a lost pet, even while saying the original pet is irreplaceable. We *talk about* pets as though losing them is a relationship loss, but we *treat* pets, in the long run, as material objects.

2. RELATIONSHIP LOSS

The first conscious awareness of relationship loss is also a childhood experience for many. It may be a loss related to moving, divorce, job change, or change in personal friendships. *Relationship loss is the ending of opportunities to relate oneself to, talk with, share experiences with, make love to, touch, settle issues with, fight with, and otherwise be in the emotional and/or physical presence of a particular other human being.*

It is an unavoidable component of human life. Sooner or later we all experience such a loss. It may be partial, as in moving five hundred miles away, or total, as with widowhood. One man recently divorced admits that what he misses most is the fights he had with his former wife. Pastoral work with those who have gone through a divorce is essentially grief counseling, though it may have other focal points as well. Relationship loss may be temporary or permanent but it always comes. Even when the relationship loss is a part of the process of growing up, it can nevertheless be a painful experience of grief.

Death ends opportunities to engage in a wide variety of forms of relating oneself to others. It is generally the most intense form of relationship loss. Death may require that a person sort through memories, address remarks to the departed person, acknowledge the pain, anger, guilt, and other feelings that may be present: in short, carry on an internal dialogue with oneself, the dead person, and others.

Just after her father's death, Joan wrote a paper entitled "A Start on Grief Work" and subtitled "Good-by, Daddy." With her permission, we reproduce part of that essay here to illustrate some of the ways people grieve relationship loss.

> My father was supposed to die two weeks before he did. His kidneys had failed. We knew there was no stopping death. The doctor guessed that death would come within a week and that it would be peaceful. He was wrong. Daddy was a fighter. As a lawyer, he won all his cases on appeal. He endured. Death came hard. He did not go gentle into that good night.
>
> When he was eight, he had to leave his family in

New York and go to a tuberculosis sanatorium in Maryland for one whole year. He was the only child there. My father never talked about that year except to say that he had spent the rest of his life trying to forget it. When he was dying, but before I was with him, my brother told me that the doctor asked him where he was, and he answered, "Maryland."

The nurse told my mother and me that last afternoon that my father was beyond feeling, that it was harder now on us than on him. On the long ride home, my mother suddenly turned to me: "I don't believe the nurse, that it's harder on us than on him. Do you?" "No." We comforted each other with realism.

(How good it was to be my father's daughter instead of one of his sons! Like a dolphin lifting his flipper, Dad showed me more often his soft side. After the funeral, my eldest brother turned to me in pained awe and said that watching Dad die was like seeing an onion peeled—and how surprised he was to find the core of his father to be sweet and soft. I accepted his discovery in silence. I had always known that. Dear God, had we had the same father?)

At the seaside funeral, my mother then called my brothers and me to her. She gave the benediction, the grace my father said on special family occasions: "Thank you, God, for the privilege of being together in this beautiful place." My brother's tears fell straight down from his eyes, making wet spots on the sand.

3. Intrapsychic Loss

Material loss and relationship loss are both likely to occur within the child's experience before adolescence. Intrapsychic loss may occur during that same period, but is more likely to happen for the first time in adolescence. It presupposes an awareness of the self present in a new way after puberty.

Intrapsychic loss is the experience of losing an emotionally important image of oneself, losing the possibilities of "what might have been," abandonment of plans for a particular future, the dying of a dream. Although often related to external experiences, it is itself an entirely inward experience. An external event may be paralleled by a significant sense of inner loss. What makes such a loss intrapsychic is that what we lose exists entirely within the self.

Very often what we lose has been a secret, a hope or a dream seldom if ever shared with others. For that reason, the fact that a loss has occurred will also be a secret. One informant notes that the first serious fight in his marriage was the occasion of intrapsychic loss. For the first few months, he had maintained an image of the marriage as perfect, largely because there had been little conflict. The first serious argument destroyed this image. The relationship continued, perhaps stronger than ever, but the image was lost, and profound sadness temporarily engulfed him. It was several years before he was able to express that experience of intrapsychic loss.

We may encounter intrapsychic loss in times of change or when a major task is successfully completed. "Buzz" Aldrin, the astronaut, referred in television interviews to the enormous sense of loss he experienced after setting foot on the moon. His life had been aimed for years at completing this task; when it was completed he found himself wondering what else there was to do. It is more common than most people realize that the completion of a task will evoke sadness.

When we claim to have lost our courage, our faith, or our grip, we are expressing intrapsychic loss. "Courage" and "faith" do not refer to objects or persons; but they are things we "have" and thus can lose. Sometimes the loss we experience is a change in perception as described in the following sketch.

I don't know what kind of loss this is, but I feel it very vividly. An uncle of mine used to visit us regularly when I was a child. I adored him. He was kind, generous, and wise. As an adolescent, I often sought his advice, and followed it, generally to my own good fortune. When I was twenty-two, I discovered that when he was twenty-two he had served a two-year term in the penitentiary. My sense of loss was devastating, and still is. He has not changed, nor has his wisdom. The change is in me.

4. FUNCTIONAL LOSS

Powerful grief can be evoked when we lose some of the muscular or neurological functions of the body; we call this functional loss. It is strongly but not exclusively associated with the aging process. Most people react with horror to the idea of a child's blindness or crippling; yet the same phenomenon in an elderly person provokes a lesser reaction, reflecting our underlying belief that functional loss naturally goes with the aging process. But loss is horrifying to young and old. Going blind at seventy-five is no less painful than going blind at fifteen even if it does happen more often.

A charming widow in her mid-seventies was playing the piano in the lounge of a retirement home. She remembered tune after tune from the 1920s and 1930s. But when asked where her son was now living, she had no idea. She simply could not remember. She remembers many lines of Shakespeare, many long-forgotten tunes, but cannot remember her own address, and usually forgets to lock her apartment door when she goes out. If someone asks her a question that she cannot answer because a portion of her memory has failed, she may become tearful and angry.

Functional loss often carries with it a loss of autonomy. To lose sight or hearing or coordination is often to lose mobility. That in turn means a loss of autonomy. Gone is the sense that "I can manage." In many cases, people will admit the fact of the functional loss but will deny that some of their autonomy is lost. Aging people whose sight is failing may admit that they have cataracts but insist that they are still perfectly capable of driving a car.

When people lose material objects, they replace them. Coping with functional loss requires a comparable "way around" a restriction or handicap. It is not uncommon to discover that persons with handicaps have invented prosthetic devices to enable themselves to live normally.

That is not always possible; and when it is not, the loss is often experienced as overwhelming. Amputation of a limb or breast, the discovery that one must wear a hearing aid, undergoing a colostomy, all these experiences are functional losses. The reaction is grief. We may be aware that a hearing-impaired acquaintance is touchy about her hearing aid or that those who use guide dogs are sometimes inappropriately angry if others admire the dog. What we may miss is that the touchiness and anger are normal grieving reactions.

5. Role Loss

The loss of a specific social role or of one's accustomed place in a social network is experienced as role loss. The significance of role loss to the individual is directly related to the extent to which one's sense of identity is linked to the lost role.

Retirement is perhaps the most familiar occasion of role loss, and for some people is accompanied by traumatic grief. But role loss can accompany experiences otherwise regarded as gains. Being promoted to a new level of responsibility at work also means a loss of freedom, and may mean losing relationships with previous friends. Priests who become bishops, skilled workers who become supervisors, and others who are promoted may experience such gains as grief-producing losses as well. Role loss is also visible when a single person marries or a married person loses a spouse. The middle-aged person who changes careers or enters school may experience loss in assuming the role of a student. The student role, with its limitations, is often acceptable if not comfortable for someone between eighteen and twenty-five, but assuming such a role at forty involves giving up other social roles; and that leads to loss and grief.

Disorientation is a powerful part of the sense of loss at this point. It involves a sense that one does not know how to behave in social situations. "How to behave" is in large part determined by the roles we have taken or have been given in a particular group. If that role disappears, we are literally without a part to play, and may indeed not know "the lines." When we are disoriented we may also sense ourselves to be at the mercy of some official or self-appointed "expert" on social behavior. A student who underwent surgery sums all this up.

> I wasn't prepared for the ways in which hospitals make people feel like nonpersons. There was a twinge when the plastic bracelet was fastened around my wrist. But what really bothered me was that when people saw that wristlet—even my friends on the staff—they immediately adopted a new tone of voice in talking to me. All of a sudden I was treated as a child.
>
> As a hospital patient you absolutely lose any control over your body and your living patterns. No matter how personal the care is in a hospital, you are fundamentally a patient, and that means you are expected, required, to take on a particular role for the comfort and convenience of the staff. Certainly taking on the patient role does not contribute to one's recovery or to successful surgery. It merely makes others feel comfortable or powerful with everybody in her own place. I was a person, a wife, a Gray Lady, a mother, a friend, a colleague, and a lot of other things before I entered the hospital. But when I became a patient I had to give up all those labels and

the roles that go with them. I was just a patient. Others had a right to touch me, move me, take me away from important companionship, leave me lying alone on a gurney in the middle of an unfamiliar hallway with no explanation, and do anything else they might decide was convenient for them. If you are a patient, you have nothing to say about any of that. Your thoughts and feelings and opinions don't count.

One of the results is that you develop very quickly a "we-they" attitude about the staff. There is a kind of mild to moderate "paranoia," in which you feel that "they" are out to get you. In practical terms, that means that you feel justified in breaking the rules, in doing whatever you can to defeat "them." They are the enemy, and lying and deceit are perfectly justified, particularly making promises that you know you have no intention of keeping.

I despair of ever making any hospital staff understand these feelings or take them seriously. I was a Gray Lady; I too had disregarded the feelings of patients, but thought I was treating them quite well.

The feelings of loss expressed here are central to our concerns. In particular, we note that to lose one's own position, to be "one-down," engenders a feeling that it is justifiable to lie, to deceive, to make promises one has no intention of keeping. The anger in such thoughts is easy to identify.

6 SYSTEMIC LOSS

Systemic loss is a concept that forced itself upon us as we studied what our informants told us. To understand it, we must first recall that human beings usually belong to some interactional system in which patterns of behavior develop over time. Even without a strongly personal relationship to others in the system, one may come to count on certain functions being performed in the system. When those functions disappear or are not performed, the system as a whole, as well as its individual members may experience systemic loss.

> Martee, one of four secretaries, enjoyed keeping her office door covered with cartoons and jokes from magazines and newspapers. Even those in the department who never worked with her took time to stop, look, and laugh.
>
> One day Martee announced that she was leaving her job and moving to San Francisco. A new secretary soon took her place. She had many of Martee's secretarial skills, and received many assignments that had been Martee's. But it was not possible to ask the new secretary to keep new jokes and cartoons posted on the door. "Martee's leaving," said another employee, "took away from us all a source of morale."

It is not surprising that one of the most common instances of systemic loss takes place when a young adult departs from the family of origin. When an individual changes or when someone leaves a family, the system must adapt to that loss. Families and other systems that have a difficult time grieving may seek to keep individuals from leaving or changing so that the system might stay the same.

> Driving home from dropping off my daughter at college for her first semester [a man writes], I experienced a great feeling of loss that she had now left our family circle, and *our family life would never be the same.* This was the first instance of one of our children reaching college age, and though intellectually I was prepared for this I found that emotionally I wasn't.

In this account we see a clear difference between relationship loss and systemic loss. To some extent, the father writing it was experiencing both. Yet he spends little time on the idea of missing his daughter himself; instead, his emphasis is on the fact that "our family life would never be the same," and he underlines the phrase to say how important it is to him. The system had undergone a loss.

COMMENT ON TYPES OF LOSS

Almost any specific loss will be a mixture of more than one of the types mentioned above. One type may predominate, but more than one type may be felt. To be widowed, for example, obviously means relationship loss. But widowhood may also mean role loss as the widow discovers that her social life has changed. She is no longer "a wife" in her community. If she has been inadequately provided for, she may undergo material loss. If her sense of identity is dependent on being her husband's wife, the change may also be experienced as intrapsychic loss.

OTHER VARIABLES IN LOSS

The type of loss is not the only variable in grief. The ways in which loss is experienced vary according to circumstances and ways in which one has learned to deal with powerful emotions. There are other variables inherent in the loss itself. These variables add to the unpredictability of grief and underscore just how many ways loss is experienced. We have chosen to focus on five.

1. AVOIDABLE AND UNAVOIDABLE LOSS

Earlier we identified many losses as unavoidable because they form a part of universal human experience. Loss itself is unavoidable. But some *particular losses* are avoidable, because they stem from having chosen a particular life-style. It is often a temptation to be unsympathetic with those whose loss is a consequence of having chosen a particular life-style.

The choice of a life-style that pays off in terms of power, influence, or financial gain carries with it comparable costs in terms of the loss of human relationships. Those who choose to be rich are often intensely lonely. In other cases, grief cannot be expressed because the relationship that has been lost was a secret. The "other" man or woman in an affair may have to hide the grief from everyone even though it is every bit as intense as the grief over a death felt by family members or "legitimate" friends.

Such losses are a matter of human choice. The loss is as great, the need as acute, and the pastor's obligation to minister as strong, in cases where society or the church disapproves of a relationship as in cases where approval is easy or certain. Although many choices involve a predictable loss, it is not always possible to foresee what the losses will be if one makes a particular choice. Dimly aware of this, some people seek to avoid ever making choices.

2. TEMPORARY AND PERMANENT LOSS

Some losses, while excruciating in their emotional effect, may be only temporary. To be able to foresee regaining what one has lost, or to know that one will eventually regain it, shapes the way in which we live our lives, and may so sharply focus attention on the lost object that other parts of life are neglected. Such was the case for a woman who waited for her husband's return from World War II.

> I went about my daily work as an accountant in a perpetual fog. Doing my job and keeping house became automatic. My entire real life—for that is how I thought of it—was focused on my husband's return from New Guinea. He was never in actual combat, and I had every reason to think that he would return safely. I call my longing for him and my pattern of writing him two letters every day my *real* life. What I did day by day, what my boss and my family saw, became *unreal*.

Knowing a particular loss is temporary may dull some of the pain. What this woman experienced was different from, but no less powerful than, the loss sustained by a woman whose husband was killed in combat. Temporary loss is also complicated by fantasies about what life will be like after "restoration." It took the writer of the illustration above almost a year to realize that her fantasies of travel with her husband would not come true; he wanted nothing more, after years in New Guinea, than to sit on his own front porch.

Permanent loss brings with it the sense that something is really ended. We may resist or avoid that knowledge, but its finality brings the necessity of making a new life without the lost person or object. To know or to imagine that a loss is only temporary, on the other hand, creates a situation in which, paradoxically, there is no end to a recurring sense of loss. Since we can imagine reunion, the intensity of longing is for some people increased by the fantasy of regaining what we have lost.

When a permanent loss seems only temporary, healthy grieving is impeded. A few years ago a well-loved pastor drowned while on vacation with his family. It was some weeks before his body was recovered. Conversations among friends involved fantasies that he was not, after all, dead. Until the body was found, a distortion was introduced into the grieving process by the fact that the loss was not established. Painful as it is, seeing the body of a dead relative or friend may assist in the development of a realistic and healing grief process.

3. ACTUAL AND IMAGINED LOSS

We have just described a situation that permitted people to imagine that a permanent loss might be only temporary. The other side of the coin: it is possible to imagine a loss where no real loss has occurred. The situation of actual versus imagined loss must be distinguished from the losses we described earlier in this chapter as intrapsychic. Since intrapsychic loss is often known only to the grieving person, others may be misled into thinking that the loss was only imagined. Not so; intrapsychic loss is just as real as any other kind. But imagined loss involves self-deception.

An elderly woman complains that her children have abandoned her. It is not true; the children are simply behaving in ways that are not in accordance with her wishes. She claims to be suffering a relationship loss ("My children never come to see me"), but the loss is not relational; the children visit her every week. What they don't do is to accede to all her wishes. Her real loss may be intrapsychic if, for example, she has always seen herself as someone whose wishes are carried out.

A more complex kind of imagined loss is the loss which we fear may take place. Lovers who are separated endure a real but temporary loss. But a lover who begins to imagine that the other no longer loves is involved in an imagined loss, one no less painful or problematic than if it were real. Such imagined losses often arise out of an earlier loss of self-esteem; if we cannot honor and care for ourselves, it is tragically easy to imagine that we are about to be abandoned by an unfaithful lover.

4. ANTICIPATED AND UNANTICIPATED LOSS

The sudden death of a loved one has an impact quite different from a death after a long and difficult illness. Bereaved persons in discussing this variable have taught us how widely feelings range. For some, a sudden loss is harder to take; for others, the sudden death of a loved one carries a small degree of comfort that the dead person did not have to suffer through a long illness.

Anticipated loss brings with it the possibility of doing some important aspects of grieving before the loss actually takes place. It provides an opportunity to "settle accounts," to renew broken or damaged relationships, and to express our pain to others, including the others we are about to lose. In the case of death, there are those who would hold back from this expression of pain in the belief that it is too great a burden for the dying person. The testimony of many dying persons is that it is no such burden at all.

5. LEAVING AND BEING LEFT

On the supposition that leaving might be a different experience from being left, we have invited members of courses and workshops on loss and grief to identify their loss experience in terms of leaving and being left. Many persons who characteristically experience separation and loss as "being left" discover that, either openly or covertly, they are hurt and angry and tend to blame the person who leaves. The underlying thought is that the leaving person has chosen to do so (even in the case of death), and is deliberately abandoning the one left. "They would not leave if they really loved us, would they?" Whether the "leaver" actually has a choice is irrelevant; the feeling of being abandoned is present.

For those who leave there is often a subtle or not-so-subtle feeling of guilt. Some people will rearrange their lives in a significant way simply to avoid the guilt of leaving. Individuals who want to quit a job may arrange to be fired; people unhappy in a marriage may seek to manipulate their partners into filing for divorce. For the leaver, there may even be an odd corner of the personality in which the leaver feels abandoned: "If you really loved me, you wouldn't let me go."

This variable is powerful when an adolescent must leave the family of origin and push on with individuation. It is no accident that family therapists list "family separation problems" as an important indication for treatment. We are impressed by the data we received when we asked students to identify significant events connected with the process of leaving home. Growing up and leaving home involves relationship loss, material loss, intrapsychic loss, systemic loss, and role loss: every form of loss but functional. We therefore believe that leaving home is one of the most powerful and critical loss events any human being undergoes.

THEOLOGICAL COMMENT

There are theological grounds to suggest that the loss of persons is of more significance than the loss of other things. It is the *human* creature that God made just a little lower than God's self, as the original version of Psalm 8 has it. In matters of life and death, the sacredness of human beings must be primary. To value things more than people or role more than personhood is a violation of God's intent for creation. Our attachment to places and things (and even ideas?) should not disrupt our commitments to and within the human community.

The unconscious does not make such distinctions. Losses derive their psychological power from the primordial loss experience. *Any* form of loss is at root experienced as a loss of a part of the self. A portion of the very fabric of our existence is ripped. The community is disrupted. The patterns of relationships that order our lives are altered.

Society does not encourage awareness of powerful loss feelings. Loss, other than the most brutal separation from those we love, is not worth worrying about, society seems to say. This is a Stoic position; it represents, in our view, one of the most powerful anti-Christian stances in present-day society. It is apathy or indifference which breeds a callous disregard for the sacredness of all life.

Loss is inescapably painful precisely because attachment is a human necessity. Our attachment to objects other than

human beings is a recognition not only that the unconscious continues to be indiscriminate throughout adulthood; it is also an affirmation of our linkage with the whole
of creation that God has given us as a sacred trust. To be
human is to be a griever for all kinds of losses.

4
The Dynamics
of Grief

Jason's wife, Marie, died suddenly in a freak home accident after a party. It had been a complicated, volatile, but satisfying marriage. Marie's unpredictability had fascinated Jason, though it disrupted the orderly world he so intensely desired. After Marie's death, Jason needed special help in coping both with his feelings and with his children.

Before moving to her new job in Helsinki, Mindy learned Swedish and Finnish well enough to manage for herself. She moved to Finland full of hope and expectation. After being in Helsinki four weeks, she felt some mild depression, but soon recovered. After six months, however, she hit a deep low, from which it took her several weeks to recover. Grief is a major aspect of adjusting to a new experience in a foreign land.

Jason and Mindy both experienced loss. Each believed that no one had ever experienced what he or she was experiencing. To some extent each was right. No two occasions of grief are ever exactly the same. Grief is always a particular response to the particular loss of a particular object. Significant difficulties exist when one attempts prematurely to identify the universal factors operating in loss and grief.

Jason's notes, written while he was beginning counseling, reveal the particularity of his grief.

> My heart feels like lead, heavy and stiff. I can't imagine that others have felt the same as I in my loss. What I feel is grief, pain, guilt, shame, desire, unrequitedness. I hurt and I ache. I have been rendered asunder. I can't stand it but I must. I need to be needed. I need to be loved. I want her so very much and she's not there. She is and was my other half. I lived in her and she in me. Can it be so wrong to have so completely absorbed her essences into me?

Marie's death was an almost lethal blow to Jason's sense of self. The loneliness he felt was compounded by a profound emptiness. Jason was sure that no one could comprehend *his* particular pain. That was one reason he kept it buried. Others might have experienced a loss, but it could not be the same. No one, he would say, could understand his grief; that insistence intensified his isolation.

Essentially, Jason was right. The anguish he felt could not be compared with any other person's grief. Jason's grief was as complicated and volatile as his marriage. It was unique. Whatever is said generally about the dynamics of grief must also include the particularity and uniqueness of each response to loss. There are, however, common themes that can and must be identified. Jason's grief was also *like* that of others.

DEFINING GRIEF

Grief is the normal but bewildering cluster of ordinary human emotions arising in response to a significant loss, intensified and complicated by the relationship to the person or the object lost. Guilt, shame, loneliness, anxiety, anger, terror, bewilderment, emptiness, profound sadness, despair, helplessness: all are part of grief and all are common to being human. Grief is the clustering of some or all of these emotions in response to loss.

In defining grief this way we agree with Erich Lindemann and others who approach grief from observation of its effects: the so-called symptomological point of view. In his landmark study of the fire at the Cocoanut Grove night club in Boston in 1942, Lindemann outlined the symptoms of normal grief, including "somatic distress, preoccupation with the image of the deceased, guilt, hostile reactions, and the loss of patterns of conduct." Lindemann observed that, in addition to these five symptoms, bereaved persons would with somewhat less frequency adopt physical symptoms or personality traits of the lost person.[14] Our own research reveals that, with one exception, all six types of loss described earlier evoke all these symptoms. (Adopting physical symptoms or traits of the lost person is only evoked by relationship loss.)

To Lindemann's list of behavior patterns, Colin Murray Parkes adds the impulse to search for the lost object. Searching has the specific aim of finding the one who is gone. That symptom is not limited to any one kind of loss. Some years ago, one of us lost a large sum of cash. To this day, he will make an occasional search of strange places in hopes of finding the money.

The alternative to regarding grief as a collection of emotions is to equate it with, or derive it from, just one emotion. David Switzer argues that the major dynamic of the inner experience of grief is anxiety, and all the behavioral responses are in some way related to this anxiety.[15] In Switzer's view, such emotions as guilt or depression or hostility may be present, but derive from anxiety. The child's hostile response to separation bespeaks anxiety about rejection.

Switzer assumes that all losses in life are a continuation of the experience of childhood separation. He argues that loss is perceived as a threat to the self because of the social character of humans. We agree. Nor can there be any doubt that anxiety or fear are always present. But we disagree with Switzer's contention that all emotions in grief are reducible to anxiety. So to reduce the feelings we experience does not give us an approach comprehensive enough to cover the almost infinite variety of loss experiences in human life. It is our intent to expand rather than to reduce the list of emotions accompanying loss in order to make sure that people experiencing loss will have the greatest possible latitude for grieving.

1. Is Grief a Disease?

Even though grief is a cluster of identifiable emotions and behaviors with a common cause, it does not fit into standard psychological classifications. It is not a functional psychiatric disorder or a subcategory of general depression or anxiety neurosis. Our intent is to maintain the ordinariness of grief. We do not regard it as a disease entity, but as the aftermath of a trauma or a temporary stress, a disorganization and confusion not unlike that which accompanies severe physical injury.

Since Freud, the psychoanalytic tradition has tended to regard grief as a disease entity. Mourning, according to Freud, is the reaction to the loss of a loved person or cherished abstraction, overcome after a period of time. It is an altogether conscious experience in which the world becomes poor and empty. Melancholia is similar in its origins, but "is bound to a condition (ambivalence) which is absent in normal grief or which, if it supervenes, transforms the latter [pathologically]."[16] The distinction between normal (unambivalent) and pathological (ambivalent) mourning would be useful were it not for the fact that the limits Freud sets are so narrow that most intense grief would have to be regarded as pathological. However, all important human relationships are ambivalent, and it is not helpful to view ambivalent grief as pathological even though the complexity of almost all losses is at first outside our awareness.

Labeling grief as a disease diminishes rather than increases our willingness to deal constructively with the pain. Grief is a part of life in a way that measles are not; to be wounded is not to be sick. To look on grief as a disease implies that finitude, loss, and death are alien to life as it was intended to be. They are not; they are an ordinary, inescapable dimension of human life.

The only advantage to labeling grief as a disease might be that if grievers thought they were sick, they might care for themselves. If grief is called an emotional or mental disease, perhaps people would not feel it so necessary to hide the "craziness of grief" that is so often present. Normal patterns *are* disrupted; people's usual coping devices do not work; they "see things" and "hear voices" and feel pains they have not felt before. Such "craziness" is standard in intense grief.

What begins as a normal response to loss may of course become abnormal. Ordinary "searching for the lost object" may become an obsession determining all of life. Withdrawal from social encounters, necessary in order to provide a space in which to grieve for a while, may become a permanent retreat from living. We often use the term "chronic grief" to refer to patterns that last too long or remain too intense. The problem with describing abnormal grief as "chronic" is that "too long" and "too intense" are subjective concepts. The uniqueness of grief makes it difficult to determine abnormality with any ease; we grieve according to our own timetables.

Even so, it is generally clear when we are ordering our lives by efforts to deny loss and hide pain. That is when grief is abnormal. Families may develop fixed patterns of interacting in an effort to minimize change and to avoid recognizing loss. They are then unable to cope with losses, which usually leads to the "storing up" of grief and its reappearance in unexpected and counterproductive forms.

> Edgar Faust, a vigorous middle-aged widower, remarried; but his second marriage seemed unsatisfying. In a consultation with their pastor, the Fausts said that their sexual life was disappointing. Mr. Faust's first wife had often told him that he was a considerate and effective lover, but he could not seem to please his new spouse. The couple discovered that the second Mrs. Faust needed more stimulation than the first, but Mr. Faust found it difficult to adjust his lovemaking to meet his new wife's needs. It was not until he took the symbolic step of visiting his first wife's grave and saying a clean good-by to her that he began to be able to be married to his new wife.

Grief is the sign of involvement and affection or, as Colin Murray Parkes puts it, "the cost of commitment."[17] When Edgar Faust discovered the depth of his love for his first wife, he was able to say good-by in a way that made it possible to commit himself to his new wife. Sometimes, however, the intensity of grief in response to some other kind of loss may exceed the grief we feel at a death. So-called minor losses may be intensely traumatic: a phonograph record, a tie, an election to a very minor job.

2. ANTICIPATED LOSS, ANTICIPATORY GRIEF

Often enough grief is caused by an unexpected loss, but at other times it is possible to anticipate an approaching loss with such intensity that one grieves as if the object were already lost. It is sometimes suggested that being able to anticipate the loss will significantly alter the grieving done once the loss takes place.

This is only partly true. Loss that occurs over a period of time may be particularly painful exactly because it is prolonged, like docking a dog's tail one inch at a time. The process of leaving a school, a job, or a community may occur over weeks and even months. Good-bys become awkward over a period of time. Friends weary of farewell parties. It is not until one turns the key in the desk for the last time or contemplates the living room empty of furniture that the loss feels final. This gradual process often feels so threatening that people avoid acknowledging it. Such avoidance works to the detriment of managing the final loss when it occurs.

> Father Martin Garnett, granted an extended study leave by his bishop, had planned not to announce his departure from his parish until the very last moment. He wanted to spare himself—he *said* he wanted to spare his parishioners—the pains of parting. Fortunately, some wiser friends insisted that some "termination work" was necessary to help his parishioners to handle the separation. They understood that Father Garnett's motivation for not telling his parishioners was very mixed, with anticipatory grief playing a large part.

The prolonged grieving process in anticipation of a final loss is common for the dying person who is leaving all the places and people that mean something to him or her. The feelings encountered in such situations are not anticipatory grief but relentless sorrow for the inability to run or sing or make love or chop wood or remember clearly. The terminally ill person is grieving in order to get ready to die, saying good-by to many things before the final loss. It is important that there be time to grieve for all that will be left behind.

The family and friends of a terminally ill person participate in some of that grief. Every "last" is cause for grieving. However, the prolonged grieving of the one who is dying and that of the survivors are not at all the same. The one dying is the primary griever; his or her losses are taking place *now*. For the survivors, anticipatory grief will occur before the final loss but it is not to be encouraged, because someone who is dying is still living. (To be sure, as a person's body and personality change, we are losing the person we knew.) Moreover, it is not possible to hold grief tightly in check, while at the same time accepting the reality of an impending death. People who are consumed with anticipatory grief have already imagined the dying person dead. The overall effect of anticipatory grieving is an intensification of isolation and loneliness.

> Luella and her father, the Colonel, admitted mother and wife Sarah to the hospital. Shortly thereafter, Sarah went into a coma. She remained comatose long enough that the Colonel and Luella began making plans for the funeral and the sale of the house. They were not prepared for eighty-two-year-old Sarah's grand reversal; she came out of the coma. Her daughter was particularly upset, saying she felt "I had done grieving that now I will have to do again." There is a caution here about anticipatory grief. Some of it is inevitable, particularly in cases like Sarah's, where the situation seems irreversible. The family's task is to allow the person to live as normally as possible without denying the seriousness of the illness. The family will have time to grieve later.

Dying and grieving cannot, therefore, be taken as identical. It is an error to imagine that the stages of dying made familiar by Elisabeth Kübler-Ross—denial, anger, bargaining, depression, and acceptance or resignation—are necessarily the stages of grieving. The one who is dying is letting go of valued and loved things and persons in order to get ready to die. Those who grieve need to let go of what has been lost *in order to get ready to live again*. Many of the dynamics will be the same, but not all. The two processes do not tend toward the same end.

THE COMMON ELEMENTS OF GRIEF

Since would-be helpers so often make the mistake of substituting their own norms for those of the grieving person, it is necessary that we be alert to the uniqueness of each person's grief. But we also need to be able to recognize the emotional components common to all grief. Despite the particularity of grief in response to a particular loss, there are certain feelings that emerge as common and significant.

There are three sources for the feelings associated with grief. The first is contemplation of the loss itself; the second is contemplation of a future without the lost object; and the third is contemplation of the unexpected experience of grief itself, i.e., feelings about grieving. The feelings that predominate when we think about the loss itself may be intensified when we realize how the loss is going to affect our relationships with other people, and the intensification of those feelings may in turn produce shock and shame at the emergence of powerful feelings we didn't know we had.

Grief is anything but systematic. The emotions discussed below are likely to occur in many unpredictable combinations depending on family attitudes toward grief, patterns of coping with stress, the specific kind of attachment we had to what we have lost, and the social acceptability we think our emotions will encounter. For convenience in discussion, we have grouped these emotions into five clusters: emptiness, loneliness, and isolation; fear and anxiety; guilt and shame; anger; and sadness and despair. But before these feelings are actively aroused in a person who has suffered a loss, there is a prior reaction that cannot quite be called an emotion, because it consists in the suppression of feeling.

1. NUMBNESS

Traumatic loss is a shock to the system. An organism faced with such a shock usually protects itself from the full impact by entering into a period of numbness. The initial dynamic of grief is most frequently an absence of feeling, a muting of affect. Accompanying this emotional state is often an insistence that the loss has not in fact occurred. As a result, a sense of unreality may pervade our interactions with others early in grief. We may insist to others that what has happened cannot have happened. In addition to this unreality, disbelief, and muted feeling, shock may also cause aimless wandering about as if the grief-stricken person were oblivious to walls or time or location.

> Although Ora and Ida McCutcheon were in their retirement years, they were, in every imaginable sense of the word, still lovers. It was a terrible blow to Ida when Ora was killed instantly in an automobile accident while taking his grandson to school. The pastor arrived at the home shortly after Ida had received the news. She was walking around the house swinging her arms wildly. "Oh! Oh!" she exclaimed. "I can't stand it. I want to die. I don't want to live without my Ora." The pastor held her in his arms, and the policeman who had brought the message washed her face. After a time she seemed to recognize the persons standing around her. Within less than an hour, the family physician came in, gave Ida a sedative, and put her to bed.
>
> Throughout the funeral service, Ida seemed half aware of her surroundings. She spoke to people and went where directed, but nothing more. After the funeral, she did not return home, saying that it was the house they had dreamed about together. Her wildness at the time of the pastor's arrival was comparable to the sudden jerk backward we may have when wounded; it was followed by a pervasive

numbness. In Ida's case, she never recovered from the numbness.

The interval between the initial shock and the return of feeling cannot be predicted. The period of numbness may last for hours or days. If there are supportive people available, the bereaved are likely to remain numb only as long as they absolutely need to. They are aware, though dimly, that there is pain soon to come. Any attempt to forestall the onset of pain defeats the organism's normal and appropriate response to trauma.

Unfortunately, that internal rhythm is not always respected. The all too common use of medication, such as the sedative Ida McCutcheon's doctor gave her, continues the numbness artificially and disrupts the normal process of grieving. The use of sedation usually causes too much time to elapse before the pains of grief are felt. Colin Murray Parkes offers a cogent caution: "While I do not doubt the efficacy of these drugs . . . the appropriateness of their use after bereavement is questionable. If, as we suppose, grief is a process of 'unlearning,' if it is necessary for the bereaved person to go through the pain of grief in order to get the grief work done, then anything that continually allows the person to avoid or suppress this pain can be expected to prolong the course of mourning. The fact remains that until the effects of tranquilizing drugs and anti-depressives have been properly assessed they should be used with caution following bereavement."[18]

The postponement caused by the use of tranquilizers will often manifest itself in abnormal grief. The length of time of intense grieving is diminished if the process of grieving can begin close to the moment of loss. Even so, there is no standard timetable for the interval between the first shock and the pains that signal the beginning of grief work. It may be minutes, hours, or days. Then the feelings begin, often with frightening intensity and surprising complexity.

2. Emptiness, Loneliness, Isolation

Emptiness is the sense of being diminished from within. Loneliness is its interpersonal counterpart, the sense that one's surroundings are also empty of people who matter or care. Isolation is the sense of being divided from others by invisible, incomprehensible boundaries. Although all these emotions are related, they may appear separately in our awareness.

People in the midst of grief express their sense of emptiness in a variety of ways. One frequently heard expression is the claim that one is only a fraction of one's former self. "I feel that three quarters of me is gone forever," Jason said. In a recent newspaper interview, Congressman Claude Pepper said of the death of his wife, "I am a ship without a rudder." C. S. Lewis, writing after his wife's death, said: "There is one place where her absence comes locally home to me, and it is a place I can't avoid. I mean my own body. It had such a different importance while it was the body of its lover. Now it's like an empty house."[19]

One's sense of self is diminished by significant loss. Because the self is partly defined by its participation in a world of attachments, loss inevitably depletes the self. This sense of self-depletion can result in a premature move to replace the lost object because we can't stand emptiness. Pastors and counselors are well aware of the intense desire of grief-stricken people to fill the "empty house" both within and without. The impulse to replace the lost person or object with a quick new attachment becomes, for some, an apparent matter of survival; they can't endure the emptiness within. Special efforts of care may be needed to help restore the self from within, so that a person does not make a new attachment he or she will later regret.

Cultural patterns also abort the process of living through the emptiness of grief. In an age of disposables and interchangeable parts, it is not easy to encourage people to feel the pain of emptiness; pressure from without as well as from within encourages them to fill the void prematurely.

Loss of any kind requires reaffirmation of the self. If one's identity was defined by the relationship with the lost person or object, then one's identity is threatened by the loss. Anxiety and depression often ensue, not because we have loved too much, but because we have loved a certain way. Human beings need autonomous centers that continue to exist even in the face of loss. We need to be attached to but not defined by others.

> Ruth, in her early forties, had established a significant, affirming relationship with Morton, the man for whom she worked. But circumstances forced the company to let her go. In reflecting on that incident later, Ruth wrote: "Because certain affirmations were never there early in my life, [building a sense of self] has been very difficult indeed. Recently I realized that because I seek identification from those I love, the lines that separate myself from another . . . have become blurred. When the relationship with Mort ended, I lost too much of my identity."
>
> Ruth's dilemma was not unusual. Significant loss always brings emptiness, but if one's identity is primarily dependent on the relationship with the lost object or person, ordinary loss becomes a profound threat.

The interpersonal counterpart of emptiness is loneliness. It is experienced in at least two ways. The loneliness of loss is to be cut off from the people we love. The loneliness of grief is the consequence of being ignored, misunderstood, and unheard. But being alone is not itself always experienced as loneliness. Those who intentionally choose to be alone are seldom if ever lonely; often they restore their sense of self through solitude. But those who are grief-stricken usually feel intensely alone, even when freed by divorce. It is even more likely to be so when the aloneness is not of one's own choosing.

When one loses a spouse, the reminders of loss are many. The bed seems larger when one sleeps alone. The house is quieter; familiar sounds are missing. Loneliness hovering in the rooms echoes the empty house of the self. The same is true when a parent or child or friend is lost. When we lose someone we love, it is the world that is depleted, and we are lonely.

The first experience of living away from home provokes a form of grief called homesickness. Homesickness includes awareness of being isolated from familiar surroundings, and a sense of being cut off from those whose presence creates community, whose absence is felt as loneliness. The intensity of feeling is sometimes surprising. Nostalgia, a word that essentially means homesickness, is built in part on a Greek root meaning "pain." It is apt. Homesickness is indeed painful.

Feelings of loneliness are heightened by the fact that others actually do tend to avoid a grief-stricken person. Friends, relatives, and helpers are often unwilling or unable to understand the intensity and complexity of grief. If no one seems to understand, or even to try, the loneliness is compounded.

In extreme circumstances, being left alone with one's grief feels like one's whole personhood is under attack. The grief-stricken person may conclude that he or she, too, should have gone away. Then at least the pain of loneliness would be over. The numbness mentioned earlier may be reinstated in an attempt to cope with pain by shutting oneself off from others.

> Ralph Cokain's wife died in June 1970. Two years later, Mr. Cokain wrote down some reflections on this theme. What he found as he looked inside himself included unexpected loneliness, a sense of

vulnerability, inferiority, and a failure of his sense of self. There were experiences he had once loved, partly because he had shared them with his wife, such as the morning paper and certain kinds of music. In the depths of his grief, he could not stand to see the morning paper or hear the music. His sense of purpose also disappeared, to be replaced by emptiness.[20]

Isolation is a necessary consequence of loss. The collapse of one's world and the erosion of internal self-certainty require some time of retreat from demanding social interaction. The grieving person feels, as did Ralph Cokain, vulnerable. We shrink from public scrutiny of our thoughts and feelings. We need a safe place to be. Isolation creates such a safe place. The invisible walls that shut out even the closest friends are sometimes necessary for a time.

Two warring needs develop: the need to be alone with one's grief and the need not to be isolated from meaningful communities of support. The Jewish custom of "sitting shiva" with grief-stricken friends comes close to bridging the gap between these two needs; one visits the bereaved person's home, sometimes without a word except a hello or good-by or shalom. Such ritual helps to protect the principal mourners from emotional invasion and unrealistic expectations. We need those rituals to regulate the chaos of grief.

Isolation may also be imposed from without. Any profound loss is a reminder of finitude to all in the vicinity, so society tends to isolate grievers in order to maintain illusions of immortality. Profound loss leads to social isolation for the same reason that those who are old or ugly are often excluded from the mainstream of human activity and interaction. Those who have experienced loss are excluded from dinner parties because their presence might "dampen our spirits" by reminding us of our own mortality. We are uncomfortable with public displays of emotion.

Being in the presence of intense emotion is awkward for most Americans (or members of most northern European societies). The grief-stricken are often indirectly told to stay home until their grief is under control.

It may be too much to expect that American society as a whole will modify those patterns, but the church could be one community where it is safe to be alone with others in grief. Sometimes there is reluctance to have a funeral in the church because we don't want to associate the church with death and loss. Similarly, people going through a divorce often isolate themselves from the worshiping community, not wanting to answer embarrassing questions. For many, church is still not an acceptable place in which to cry. That is both socially unfortunate and theologically unsound.

3. Fear and Anxiety

Fear and anxiety are experienced as part of grief in three ways: the dread of abandonment; the anxiety of separation; and fear of future contingencies. The first two are sometimes thought of as the same thing, but we believe that keeping them separate is useful.

The Dread of Abandonment

The infant's helpless dependence for well-being on the mothering one's care means that being cut off from that care—especially if it happens prematurely—is the beginning of the dread of abandonment. That dread lingers throughout life as an awareness of nonbeing which we can tolerate only in small doses. To be abandoned is not to *be*. These memories of beginning life influence and even direct our responses to attachment and loss later. Experiencing abandonment recapitulates earlier helplessness.

> Earlier, we told a story of a woman named Carrie, who was devastated after the death of her grandfa- ther. It was for Carrie a profound experience of

abandonment. The only family member who she believed loved her—her grandfather—had irrevocably left her. She knew how deeply she feared being abandoned. "I was crushed. I loved my grandfather. I had seen some deaths, but his death was the first one in which I was involved personally. And I was abandoned. I fled the hospital, got into my Volkswagen, and roamed the streets helplessly."

Her relationship with her grandfather had provided Carrie with a stable environment. When she was hit with the death of this single provider of stability, she relived a primordial experience of helplessness. Death is by no means the only experience that can do this to us. Radical changes in life-style or sudden separations often evoke this same dread.

The utter desolation of the words of Jesus from the cross, "Eli, Eli, lama sabachthani?" ("My God, my God, why hast thou forsaken me?"), is a reflection of the desolation of a psalmist in Israel. Both the psalmist and Jesus express the anguish of being abandoned. "Don't go away" is the haunting plea of someone terrified at being left alone. There are few things in life more painful. A lost child's panic at the fair or in a huge department store, multiplied many times over, begins to get at the sense of forsakenness. It involves not only utter helplessness but the feeling that the very ground we stand on is caving in under us.

The Anxiety of Separation

Similar to the dread of abandonment, separation anxiety refers to the sense of threat to one's own survival as a *self*. Because we are social creatures, the loss of someone or something we love is experienced as a threat to the self. If we think, consciously or not, that a loss will seriously deplete the self, we become anxious. The greater the emotional investment in the lost person or object, the greater the possibility of such anxiety. Not all grief can be reduced to anxiety; but if the grieving person was excessively dependent on the lost person or object for self-definition, then anxiety about oneself may in fact be the most observable aspect of grief.

In her helpful book, *Death and the Family*, Lily Pincus outlines the consequences, particularly for women, of depending for one's identity upon the attachment to spouse or parent or child.[21] Normal maturing involves a shift from dependence to autonomy. For the autonomous individual, loss evokes less anxiety about one's survival. But not everyone matures according to this "normal" design. When separation or loss seems to generate terror, it indicates that included in the work of grieving will need to be some reconstruction of the self.

> So it was for Cynthia in her grief. As a child she had borrowed identity and worth from her father. After marriage she spent thirty-seven years concerned for her husband's health, career, and success. Though talented and competent herself, Cynthia set herself aside for the man she loved. When he was dying, she longed to put aside her life for his.
>
> "When I learned that Ralph might not survive the operation," she wrote, "I would have been willing to be put to sleep, have my heart taken out and give it to Ralph if that would help. All I could think was, 'This man must not die.' My husband should live, and it does not matter if I do or not. . . . Am I really nothing to people without Ralph? Am I not loved for myself, liked for myself, or even respected for myself by anyone?"
>
> When Ralph died, Cynthia lost the source of her identity. Afterward, she was never quite able to discover her own sense of self. Finding a photograph in a drawer, meeting a mutual friend, waking up alone in a double bed all would precipitate attacks of what Parkes calls anxious pining—the subjective, inward aspect of the urge to search for the lost object.

Other species demonstrate this tendency sharply. When the greylag goose is separated from its mate, it makes immediate, anxious attempts to find the mate again. It goes restlessly on searching expeditions, visiting each place where the partner might be found and uttering constantly a special "long-distance" call. Cynthia's behavior and inner state were markedly similar, as a result of her profound, self-depleting loss.

Since separation provokes fear and anxiety, it is not surprising that it is often accompanied by sighing, shortness of breath, and fatigue. There may also be "phantom pain," actual, usually fleeting pain with no apparent cause.

Fear of the Future

Anxiety is usually vague and unfocused. But fear in response to loss is conscious, concrete, and focused. In her candid book *Widow*, Lynn Caine describes the beginning of her grief: "When the protective fog of numbness had finally dissipated, life became truly terrifying. I was full of grief, choked with unshed tears, overwhelmed by the responsibility of bringing up two children alone, panicked about my financial situation, almost immobilized by the stomach-wrenching, head-splitting pain of realizing that I was alone. My psychic pain was such that putting a load of dirty clothes in the washing machine, taking out the vacuum cleaner, making up a grocery list, all the utterly routine household chores, loomed like Herculean labors."[22]

Lynn Caine is able to identify immediate and concrete fears. It is frightening to be deprived of whatever or whomever we have come to rely on for encouragement, support, and confidence to face the world. It may sometimes be a very small thing. A recently divorced man described feelings of uncertainty when he discovered how accustomed he was to tapping his wedding ring on the steering wheel as he drove. He was amazed by the uncertainty that accompanied the absence of this familiar item and the gesture that went with it.

Divorced persons are often afraid of being attractive. Uncertainty about functioning in a new role or setting is evoked by a change from what was familiar. Being lost and alone in a strange place can produce profound panic. Even a temporary separation from familiar routine can be intolerable.

The unfamiliar feelings that go with grief can themselves produce fear. When the grief is intense or marked by unusual behavior (such as searching for the lost object or hearing voices) one may quickly come to doubt one's sanity. It is reassuring to discover that there is a kind of normal craziness to grief. Lynn Caine writes: "I was idiotically inconsistent. I swung from outlandish attempts to solve my problems . . . to maudlin, childish endeavors to set the clock back and try to pick up the threads of my life from the years before I knew Martin. Few of my actions had much to do with reality. They were freakish, inconsistent. Crazy."[23]

It is important to provide some protective space so that grief-stricken people can temporarily "have their craziness" without acting in ways that further complicate the grief. For someone who has suffered a major loss, there is nothing shameful or, in the long run, fearful about the craziness of grief. Those "crazy impulses" may be strong even when the loss seems trivial to outsiders.

> Fred (sixteen) broke up with his girl friend of three months. His home life was stable and loving, even though the family had not yet adjusted fully to mother's full-time employment.
>
> When Janine told Fred that she wanted to be free to go out with other boys and not be exclusively tied to him, he was determined to "take it like a man." Even so, he invented excuse after excuse to walk or drive

down Janine's block. His brother noticed and, as brothers will, teased Fred unmercifully. Fred flew into a white-faced rage, but later apologized for his "crazy" behavior.

Those who know adolescents know how common such incidents are; they also understand how seriously they are taken at the time. What may have been overlooked in this instance was that Fred sensed a number of losses; his grief was marked by the anxious pining mentioned above.

4. Guilt and Shame

Some years after both her parents had died, a young woman wrote a letter and read it aloud at her father's grave. Her pastor had recommended such action in an effort to unlock the guilt she had carried for her mother's death, for which her father had accused her of being responsible. What she wrote to her father was heavily laced with the anger at oneself that often accompanies guilt and shame.

> I'm tired of being pushed around. I'm tired of people trying to make me into something I can't and don't want to be. I'm tired of taking the blame for other people's illnesses. You blamed me for Mom's sickness. I remember you coming into the room to which I had retreated in rage and frustration. You came there after me and said, "It's your fault that your mother is so sick. It's no wonder that she's sick with you upsetting her so much." Dad, did you ever have any idea of how much you hurt and frightened me with those words? Somehow you must have known you were wrong—and you were wrong. It is not my fault that she got sick and died! I don't have the power to cause or determine whether someone will be sick or not or live or die. I'm just me and that's all I ever wanted you to see and accept and love.

Guilt is a dominant component of grief. It results from three combined factors: assuming responsibility for an individual loss; decisions that may have hastened or contributed to the loss; and residue from the relationship with the lost person or object. On occasion, people feel guilt for being relieved that a lingering illness has ended at last or a miserable marriage is finally over. Most of the guilt associated with grief is useless and counterproductive to constructive grieving. In some instances guilt comes as an unconsciously motivated punishment for being the one who survived. In other instances, people feel guilty about the grief itself: a consequence of moralistic attitudes toward the normal human response to loss.

The impulse that produces the most immediate guilt involves taking responsibility for the loss. In the case of death grief-stricken persons are sometimes inclined to heap coals of fire on their own heads for presumed negligence. "If only" punctuates a litany of guilt. "If only I had not left the room." "If only we had gone to see one more specialist." "If only we'd insisted that Dad retire." All these "if onlys" presume that the disaster could have been averted or at least postponed if something else had been done. A woman in her sixties discusses her release from such guilt after an adult education class in church.

> After my mother's death I told myself that it was all my fault, because I could not insist that she stay flat on her back. The doctors said that she would die in a year if she lived a relatively normal life and that is just what she did. And then you helped me to realize that it was her life, and that she lived and died as she chose. It was even arrogant of me to assume that I had any right to make the choice for her. After thirty-five years, I was finally free from guilt.

To be sure, there are instances of negligence that hastens death, but in most cases the survivor's guilt is either exaggerated or unnecessary. This is particularly true when there has been a suicide. Two years after her son had committed suicide, May Carlson was still berating herself for not having seen the signs of his distress. "I am a nurse," she said. "I should have known." Overwhelmed by guilt, she was kept from realizing that even if she had read all the signs correctly, it was unlikely that she could have prevented her son's suicide. Giving up guilt requires a recognition of the limits to human responsibility.

Guilt is often related to wishes, expressed or unexpressed. Even as adults, the child in us believes that wishes are magic; that they have the power to make things happen. If a child wishes someone dead, and that person does die, the child will easily believe that she or he has made it happen by the magic of wishing. In early adolescence, Sandra sometimes wished that her alcoholic father would die so she would not have to be ashamed to have friends come to her house. Fourteen years after her alcoholic father committed suicide, Sandra had not spent her social security benefit. She regards it as blood money. When children are excluded from the funeral they may conclude it really was their fault that the death occurred. It is not surprising, then, that a child's grief over the death of someone he or she loved is often complicated by hidden guilt. Children should not be excluded from conversations at the time of death or from funeral activities, if for no other reason than to prevent guilt for those secret wishes that they—and we—may believe have magical power.

A relationship does not have to be troubled for guilt to enter. A businessman of our acquaintance often thought that his superior, a close friend and longtime companion, was making serious mistakes in judgment. "If I were the department director," he said to himself, "I'd run things differently." His friend died; he was promoted. As department director he was at first quite ineffective. "Until I realized that my guilt was unnecessary," he told us, "it just about undid me." It is as if we must believe that death is an alien force. Belief in magic assumes that wishing can influence that alien power of death.

Advances in medical technology have increased the likelihood of someone's having to take responsibility for decisions that will either hasten or prolong another person's dying. Such responsibility usually falls on members of the patient's immediate family. Irreversible life-and-death decisions are inevitably laden with terrifying ambiguity. Many people have developed an "ethical system" based on avoiding guilt; they usually decide to prolong life in order to avoid feeling guilty.

A seventy-four-year-old woman insisted on keeping her ninety-four-year-old mother at home at great personal cost. She cared for her incoherent and incontinent mother with affection and great devotion, but also so that no one could say, and she would never feel, that she had shirked her duty. The elaborate efforts that some people undertake in order to avoid guilt produce, in turn, anger at the deceased loved one for taking so long to die. Such angry feelings may be denied, and prompt added guilt.

Guilt is not a consequence of making decisions so much as it is a consequence of false theological assumptions. The "ethical system" built on the assumption that if we simply try hard enough we can avoid sin is no ethical system at all. All ethical choices are surrounded by ambiguity. And yet, as Christians we are called to act responsibly. Such a call cannot save us from errors of judgment or even unclear motives. Unless there is recognition of the ambiguity of all human choice, and a capacity to live with that ambiguity, advances in medical technology are likely to intensify the guilt involved in grief.

In divorce, guilt can be a major impediment to effectively grieving the end of a marriage. Years ago, clergy of many denominations were free to remarry a divorced person so long as he or she was the "innocent" party to the divorce.

It is now generally agreed that there is no such thing as an innocent party. Both parties are always partly accountable in a divorce. Still the false notion of innocence lives on. Couples are reluctant to examine why their marriage has ended because each party is intent on maintaining the position of innocent victim. This sabotages the process of working through the end of a marriage in a way that will foster growth.

Sometimes what looks like guilt is really shame: shame at being a griever. Grieving persons sometimes express great embarrassment about their condition. C. S. Lewis put it candidly: "An odd by-product of my loss is that I'm aware of being an embarrassment to everyone I meet. . . . Perhaps the bereaved ought to be isolated in special settlements like lepers."[24]

Feelings of shame for grieving do not merely spring from within; society isolates those who mourn by supporting feelings of shame about grieving.

> A psychiatrist working in an institution that served retarded children lost his wife after a long illness. His colleagues avoided him, mumbling condolences that did not add up to a full English sentence. It was a great relief to him when a retarded boy bluntly said to him, "Doctor, your wife died." "Yes," responded the psychiatrist. "That must hurt a lot," said the boy. The doctor later commented that it was a profound and helpful remark, in contrast to the responses of his friends.

Because grief is by its nature excessive and unpredictable, it may erupt at awkward moments: at lunch, taking dictation, singing in the church choir. So as not to be an embarrassment to friends, the grieving person may hide the pain from others or from himself or herself. People also feel shame when their grief does not follow what they have come to regard as a standard timetable. "I shouldn't be crying this way," they say, as if the statute of limitations on grieving had run out. Shame is an unnecessary component of grieving, but is often imposed by society's unwillingness to grant permission to grieve.

5. ANGER

Even under the most normal circumstances anger is complex and difficult to handle. Accepting, managing, and expressing anger as a part of grief is complicated by both personal discomfort and social taboo. *De mortuis nil nisi bonum* means, loosely translated, "Don't speak ill of the dead." When the loss is a death, the anger is usually directed away from the deceased and toward family members, medical personnel, or God. In other loss the anger is often much more visible and much more often aimed at the lost object. Nonetheless anger is an immediate, common, and inevitable response to loss. Anger with a lost loved one is an integral part of grief.

Angry protest is, according to John Bowlby, the first phase of response to separation. For the small child protest is generally a vigorous attempt to recapture mother by any means possible. A dying adult may protest in the form of a raging plea not to be abandoned. Even though such expressions of anger may be hopeless and unrealistic, they are a necessary precondition for mourning to run its course. "Protest, including an angry demand for the person's return and reproach against him or her for deserting, is as much a part of an adult's response to loss, especially a sudden loss, as of a young child's."[25]

Since it is irrational, such anger is also indiscriminate in its targets. It may be directed at little Johnny, whose yelling from the back porch "made" mother drop the porcelain vase she was cleaning. The last visitor talked too much; the pastor prayed too long; the children demanded too much attention; the neighbors should have known enough to call when they saw the dog off the leash. Such responses seek to fix blame for the loss. Traumatic loss upsets our illusion that we live in an orderly world. If we can find someone or something to blame, we can continue to avoid the fact that life is uncertain and precarious.

Our rage against God for allowing a tragedy to happen is predicated on the primordial conviction that at least God can stop the spread of a tumor or an infestation of fruit flies or children from moving too far away. If God is in control, why does he allow tumors to spread or trains to crash? Perhaps God is impotent and not in control after all or is, in the language of C. S. Lewis, a "cosmic sadist." Lewis' unexpurgated anger at God is an inescapable component of his grief: "If God's goodness is inconsistent with hurting us, then either God is not good or there is no God: for in the only life we know He hurts us beyond our worst fears and beyond all we can imagine. . . . Step by step we were led 'up the garden path.' Time after time, when He seemed most gracious He was really preparing the next torture."[26]

God is neither the cause of suffering nor a capricious sadist plotting our pain. But the mystery of loss is part of the pain of grief. Knowing that it is indeed a mystery did not prevent Lewis, nor should it prevent us, from scolding God in our grief. Raging at God is a part of the Hebrew tradition. The psalms of lament are filled with anger at God for God's absence and seeming disregard for the plight of God's people. Anger, especially as a part of grief, is not contrary to faith or faithfulness, but an inescapable response to loss.[27]

Even so, because anger is such an embarrassing emotion, and so often unwelcome, we seldom allow ourselves to experience it cleanly or to aim it at its true object. Instead, we kick the dog for something the boss said; we pummel a racquetball because we failed an assignment; or we turn our anger inward upon ourselves. When mourners are not raging at God or the medical profession, they are often looking for a chance to castigate themselves for some minor omission or negligent word. Since anger is a part of the grief, it must find some release if mourning is to take its proper course.

Sometimes the anger in grief evokes such guilt that the bereaved glorify the lost object unrealistically. Speaking only of the goodness of the deceased and ignoring her or his negative attributes may function to reassure the mourner that the dead person is worth grieving for. Idealizing the dead does not eliminate ambivalence; it merely sends it "underground," making it harder to deal with. The internalized image that we carry in memory after a loss should correspond closely to the ordinary, wonderful, flawed person we loved. Pastors can often help by privately and publicly remembering that lost person "warts and all."

There are two seemingly opposite but deeply related ways of mishandling anger in connection with grief. We can dwell on the anger, nurse it along, let it become the major preoccupation of the mind. Or we can refuse to consider anger, refuse to recognize it when it emerges, reject it as abnormal. In either case, the griever is being dominated by anger. In the first instance, anger is such a visible phenomenon that it is easy to see that it dominates the mourner. In the second instance, the mourner spends so much emotional energy coping with anger, repressing it, that it also truly dominates the personality.

6. SADNESS AND DESPAIR

Sadness is a normal, healthy response to any misfortune. "Most, if not all, . . . intense episodes of sadness," says John Bowlby, "are elicited by the loss, or expected loss, either of a loved person or else of familiar and loved places and social roles. A sad person knows who or what he has lost, and yearns for his (or its) return."[28] Sadness can range from momentary distress over the loss of an election to the deep sadness felt over the death of a spouse.

When sorrow is coupled with fear and a sense of futility about the future, that is despair. We generally reserve despair to describe a loss that darkens the prospects for a meaningful future.

Sadness and despair are normal aspects of acute grief, but not easy for those around the griever to tolerate. Well-meaning efforts to help are often rejected as pointless. The person feels alone and bereft in the world, consumed by a sense of hopelessness. In such a state, it is common for the grieving person to be preoccupied with an image of the lost object; that preoccupation in turn deepens the sense of helplessness. Life seems monstrous. Deep despair is not necessarily present in all grief; but when it is present, it is a normal, appropriate response to traumatic loss.

7. SOMATIZATION

Up to this point we have considered grief in terms of its emotional components; the emotions that underlie the distress. But there are also physical components. Physiological symptoms are also caused by grief, and may be quite powerful. Lindemann has identified somatic signs common in acute grief: "Sensations of somatic distress occurring in waves lasting from twenty minutes to an hour at a time, a feeling of tightness in the throat, choking with shortness of breath, need for sighing, an empty feeling in the abdomen, lack of muscular power, and an intense subjective distress described as tension or mental pain."[29]

Bereavement affects one's physical well-being. Headaches, insomnia, loss of appetite, weight loss, fatigue, dizziness, and indigestion, are all common to the experience of grief. Unless they persist in an intensified way, these somatic and behavioral symptoms should be regarded as normal. The whole of one's being grieves a loss. It should not be surprising that people report that their bones ache, their hearts throb, and their bowels are in ferment. These same symptoms are recorded in the thirtieth chapter of The Book of Job: "By night pain pierces my very bones, and there is ceaseless throbbing in my veins" (Job 30:17, NEB). Two phenomena often associated with acute grief are physical pain in one's limbs and sleep disturbance. The sleep disturbance is so common that one could almost call it universal; the limb pain is less common but still frequent. The pain, which is not actually in the bones but the muscles, is apparently the result of muscular tension associated with repressed feelings.

Job 30 records many more physical symptoms, and some emotional concomitants of acute grief, as well. Early in the chapter we find suggestions of resentment and anger at others, hints that Job sees himself as isolated even when others are trying to help. The chapter is a poetic description of one man's experience, but it echoes the phenomena reported by thousands of sufferers since Old Testament times.

THE UNIQUENESS OF GRIEF

Whatever is said about grief in general must be understood in the light of the fact that each instance is unique. Grief is a particular response to a particular loss of a particular relationship at a particular time. The form that a particular instance of grief takes is shaped by a number of factors.

1. INTENSITY OF ATTACHMENT
The intensity of the attachment that we have to a lost person or an object is a major factor. That intensity is essentially unrelated to the length of time we have been involved with the person. Attachment has to do with an investment of the self. The person or object becomes a part of our inner world, and so the loss will deplete our very self.

That intensity is most often built on an identification of

the mourner with the object that has been lost. But the identification may be based on acquaintance of anywhere from ten minutes to a lifetime. Thus, the intensity is not easy to predict, and may be surprising to mourners and those around them alike.

2. COMPLEXITY OF ATTACHMENT

We have indicated already that attachments may have a strong positive meaning, a strong negative meaning, or a mix of the two. The form grief takes in a particular instance is determined in part by the mix of positive and negative feelings in the now broken attachment. That grief is always unique to a particular situation becomes less and less surprising.

> When Horst Heck's wife Lieselotte was killed, Horst went into seclusion. As one of their sons put it, "It was as if someone had turned off a switch in Dad's brain." Horst stopped having anything to do with other people. His relationship with Lieselotte was complex. He was not only deeply attached to her; he was far more dependent on her than he or she ever knew. Although his business had seemed under his control, he actually made no decisions without his wife's approval. The pattern had unusual power because neither acknowledged that he was asking for approval and she was giving or withholding it. His behavior after her death puzzled others because no one had known the complexity of Horst's attachment to his wife.

THE UNPREDICTABILITY OF GRIEF

If grief in any given instance is unique, it follows that it is unpredictable. The nature of our attachment to a person or object is often formed without conscious awareness. It is therefore difficult to anticipate the intensity or the complexity of grief. People living together in a family may surprise one another by their widely varying reactions to the same loss. To the dismay of the parents, the heartbreak of a child whose puppy is killed may be more intense and profound than his or her grief for the death of an aged grandparent. The emotional value of an object is often unknown until it is lost.

> Pastor Schmidt dropped in to see Mrs. McCann, an eighty-six-year-old woman whose middle-aged grandson had died suddenly the previous week. Her daughter, the dead man's mother, was also present. Despite Pastor Schmidt's efforts to engage the younger woman in conversation about the death of her son, Mrs. McCann constantly interrupted to lament her inability to drive a car. Seemingly insensitive to her grandson's death and her daughter's needs, the aged woman was expressing her pain at the loss of mobility and freedom. Her grieving was understandable, but it did not fit a predictable pattern.

Recognition of the unpredictability of grief leads to the realization that it is not useful to define grief in terms of stages except in the broadest possible way. The fact that a particular person expresses feelings in a way we had never anticipated or encountered must not be allowed to mislead us into thinking that that person's grief is in any way abnormal. Generalizing about grief is likely to inhibit the full expression of grief because it cancels our particularity.

Maintaining a balance between the general and the particular is essential for the effective care of mourners. Unfortunately, some people intentionally generalize about a loss in order to counteract the so-called selfishness of grief. Their desire is to turn grieving persons away from themselves on the grounds that such preoccupation is both emotionally destructive and theologically inappropriate. There *is* a danger that an exclusive focus on the uniqueness of grief could result in self-encapsulation. Persons who mourn eventually need to see their loss in the larger perspective of human finitude and suffering. But at that point the purpose of generalizing is to help them make sense of their experience, not to restrict the supposed excesses of feeling.

In his *Letters of Spiritual Counsel*, Luther illustrates the tension between the general and the particular. On the other hand, Luther encourages others toward the full expression of their pain. In a long letter to Benedict Pauli, a jurist and burgomaster in Wittenberg, he acknowledges Pauli's grief over the death of a son. In the next paragraph, however, he counsels moderation and control of Pauli's grief, by listing patriarchs of faith who suffered even greater loss. "If you reflect on these and similar examples, you will understand that your misfortune is not at all to be compared with even a part of the misfortune and grief of those men, and by this comparison your own grief will be greatly relieved and lightened."[30] Luther is quick to shift the focus away from a particular sorrow to human suffering in general and to the suffering of Christ which is greater than all other. Luther's intent is comfort and moderation, but the effect is more one of control than one of comfort. The shift is delicate. Too much emphasis on particularity leads to stultifying self-absorption. Generalizing, on the other hand, invalidates an individual whose grief is always particular. For those who care, movement from the particular to the general requires sensitive timing, so as not to cancel out the feelings of the individual, whose grief is always unique.

5
The Characteristics
of Grieving

Grief is the inevitable response to significant loss; there is no loss without grief. It is possible, however, not to *grieve*. One may choose not to express the feelings that accompany loss. When that happens, grieving is delayed and the grief is "stored up," with unfortunate consequences. Not that grieving is any more predictable than grief. It is a process that shows itself in many different forms. Some of them can be labeled healthy or unhealthy, normal or abnormal, but the most fruitful set of labels may be successful or unsuccessful. Because there are so many internal and external variables that impinge on grieving, it is rather risky to use a phrase such as "normal grieving."

Grieving is a process moving toward a receding goal, a goal never fully reached; the relative "normality" of the process is judged by its effectiveness in helping the grieving person to approach that goal as closely as possible. The goals of grieving include these: to enable a person to live a life relatively unencumbered by attachments to the person or thing lost; to remake emotional attachments; to recognize and live with the reality of the loss and the feelings occasioned by it. Moving toward these goals can involve a variety of activities, and any activity that moves one in this direction is "normal."

SHAPES OF GRIEVING

Despite the fact that there are many variables to the process, there are several activities so common that we have labeled them "shapes of grieving." Some are intentional or semi-intentional; others are phenomena that tend to happen when a person is working on grieving; they serve as evidence that the process is going on.

1. SEARCHING FOR THE LOST OBJECT

Searching is a common pattern in grieving. Ethological studies have identified the impulse to recover (and to scold!) as common among both human and nonhuman species. It is usual to search for what is lost even when at some level we are aware that it is irretrievably gone. Not surprisingly, the searching sometimes results in a kind of finding. People undergoing acute grief may live with a sense of the continued presence of the deceased, a sense of his or her being near. Not unlike the transitional object of infancy and childhood, the sense of a lost person's presence is a way of coping with the pain of separation. Cynthia, to whose loss of her husband we have previously referred, wrote this vignette.

> "I was, as usual, in his study reading (about 2 A.M.) and suddenly I had to walk. I got as far as Sycamore Avenue, and there he was. What do I mean 'there he was'? It was as if I had to stop and turn toward him standing by me, and I opened my arms as did whatever power or spirit of Ralph. I stood in the middle of a dark street with my arms open. As nearly as one can I had the feeling of embracing someone with a nonexistent body. Just as he turned to me that way and I spoke to him, my arms finally fell to my sides empty, for there was no one really there."

Later Cynthia thought she saw her husband again,

but that was the last visual appearance. Her grieving then turned in another direction as she sought to replace her lost love. That in itself is significant; the visual appearances ended. If they had continued, it would have been evidence that problems of fixation on the lost object had arisen.

Notice that searching for the lost object goes on in the *present*, as though the lost person were still around just waiting to be seen or found. The grieving person is able to admit without difficulty that time has passed since the loss. This fact distinguishes searching from a phenomenon we call "time-freezing," in which the passage of time is denied, or the grief-stricken person attempts to stop time (symbolically or really) in its flight. Time-freezing is an attempt to dwell on, or in some cases actually to live in, the time just prior to the loss. Quite often this takes the form of keeping a room or a portion of the house just as it was when the loved one was still present, or remembering only the last meeting.

Human minds have ways of warding off unwelcome experience, called "defense mechanisms." The behavior we are discussing here is evidence of the defense mechanism called *denial*. The loss may be admitted intellectually, but the person behaves as if the loss had not taken place or, in some cases, as though it were reparable. (This latter defense is *undoing* rather than denial.) The denial or undoing may be restricted to one aspect of life or one physical area of the house but colors all of life indirectly. The underlying defenses remind us that these phenomena can easily become abnormal. If, at a deep emotional level, the person who has suffered a loss denies the reality of that loss, the process of letting go is severely compromised.

Theologically speaking, the impulse to search for what is lost is a faithful response, but time-freezing is an unfaithful response. Job describes his pain and anger in vivid detail, but ultimately engages in no denial. "The Lord gave," he says, "and the Lord has taken away." (What a terrible arrogance it is if anyone but a griever speaks that line!) "Even if he kills me, I trust him." But those who keep a room ready for their son, killed in Vietnam, to occupy on his return, are engaging in an unfaithful response. They are unwilling to acknowledge the reality of their situation. And because they do not accept that reality, their lives are ordered by death rather than by God who is always making something new.

2. IMMODERATION

Grieving cannot be done in controlled doses at scheduled times; it is essentially immoderate. Just as the loss itself is usually experienced as breaking in upon us (even when we may have been expecting it), so the feelings of grief are experienced as invading us suddenly, sometimes when we least expect them. An image or a memory strikes suddenly, opening the door to a flood of feelings that we suppress at our peril.

For prudential reasons, a grieving person may choose not to let feelings show in some situations, but we need not try to make them go away. An elderly widow, who all her life had a strong investment in keeping her feelings under control, was heard muttering angrily to herself. When asked why she was berating herself, she said that feelings of grief over the death of her husband kept recurring, and she did not want to have them. She thought such powerful feelings three years after her husband's death were evidence of something wrong with her. She was somewhat relieved when told that her feelings were quite to be expected.

Grieving is a disorderly process; in the midst of acute grief the usual means of controlling our feelings and our surroundings simply do not work.

> When Jim Eccles was nineteen and a sophomore in
> college, he took some of his cherished classical record

collection to school. A redcap picked up the container of records, found it unexpectedly heavy, and dropped it. Only one record was broken, but it was irreplaceable; RCA Victor was no longer making or selling it. From that time on, Jim could not hear that piece of music without experiencing strong sadness and anger. When, some years later, RCA Victor reissued the performance on long-playing records, Jim immediately bought a record and left the store without waiting for change from his ten-dollar bill. None of his behavior was particularly rational; all of it was understandable.

Luther admonished his followers that grief *should* be moderate. His approach to traumatic loss has been dominant in many Christian traditions. To Benedict Pauli he wrote: "The Scriptures do not prohibit mourning and grieving over deceased children. . . . Nevertheless, there ought to be a certain moderation in our grief."[31] Luther's reason for such an approach is twofold: excessive grieving leaves no room for consolation; and uncontrolled sorrow may lead the believer to lose sight of the cross in comparison to which all our crosses are light or as nothing.

Luther sees a truth at this point, but draws an erroneous conclusion. He understands that if we grieve deeply, we shall for the moment not be able to see God's suffering in Christ. The problem with Luther's admonition is that not to grieve deeply is to grieve inadequately, distortedly. Premature consolation is pointless when people are filled with sorrow. To quell the grieving is not to stop the storm at sea, but merely to build a wall so that we do not see the storm or its effects. Freedom to grieve intensively from the onset of loss is what makes space later for a remembrance of Christ's suffering and a reaffirmation of the loving will of God that seemed so strange when the pains of grief were acute.

3. Grieving Is Spiral, Not Linear

A model displaying the shape of grieving might take the shape of a spiral figure. The spiral would begin at a low point representing the emotional "low" brought on by loss, and would move circularly upward as the griever climbed out of the "pit." But from time to time the spiral would bring the mourner to a point directly above the beginning low point; that is a moment when many of the intense feelings would suddenly return. (Such a point often comes on an anniversary of some kind: the day someone died, a birthday, Thanksgiving, Christmas.)

At the end of his third notebook and the beginning of the fourth, when his rage had diminished and he had begun to "feel better," C. S. Lewis felt all the hells of his young grief again: the mad words, the bitter resentment, the fluttering in the stomach, the nightmare unreality, the tears and the wallowing in them. Am I going in circles, he asks, or dare I hope that I am on a spiral? "Grief is like a long, winding valley where any bend may reveal a totally new landscape. As I've already noted, not every bend does. Sometimes the surprise is the opposite one: you are presented with exactly the same sort of country you thought you had left behind miles ago. That is when you ponder whether the valley isn't a circular trench. But it isn't. There are partial recurrences, but the sequence doesn't repeat."[32]

A linear model inadequately represents grieving as a straight line aimed for a definite place. It suggests that one can in fact leave the loss behind cleanly and completely, and this is simply not the case. The farther one "climbs out" (to use the spiral model), the less power the loss has, but it never loses its power entirely.

A linear model manages to suggest that the griever should be at a particular point at a particular time, and that after Feeling X must always come Feeling Y. Such suggestions merely add to the frequent sense of shame felt by grieving persons when they experience the unexpected return of intense feelings. The spiral model serves better to promote genuine freedom to feel one's feelings. The powerful loss, never completely left behind, may be rediscovered around the next corner. By the grace of God, our losses become a spiraling part of life which enriches even as we once felt it diminished us.

4. TIME DISTORTION

In grieving we often distort our sense of time. At points, time seems to pass more quickly than usual; at other points, far more slowly. Concepts such as past and future tend to lose their meaning in the first acute reaction to loss. The bereaved have great difficulty in getting past the moment of death, or the last time the lost person was seen. All the past is temporarily collapsed into that moment, and it feels as if there were no other past. Nor is there a future. The calendar is not advanced to the next month. "I can't think that far ahead," a grieving person will say. Taking life "one day at a time" means for the bereaved being locked into the present or the immediate past. The deceased is referred to in the present tense of verbs, partly out of habit but partly so as not to acknowledge fully and consciously the loss that has taken place. It is a way of staying close to the lost object. This is the phenomenon that can turn quickly into the time-freezing we discussed earlier.

When grieving people allow themselves to be stuck at a particular moment in time without either past or future, the process becomes stuck. In order to assist in the painful process of embracing a future without the lost object, we will suggest that an alternation between remembering and hoping is the proper central focus of work with those who grieve. The degree to which individuals have shut out the past is proportional to their inability to imagine a future. Reminiscing is intended to liberate the bereaved from emotional claims of the past in order to think hopefully about the future.

5. GRIEVING IS SELF-ORIENTED

The impulse to turn in upon oneself to the exclusion of others is commonplace in grieving. Such behavior is not unlike the detachment described by John Bowlby, which we mentioned earlier, as a characteristic response of the child to the process of separation. Turning inward in grief may be as necessary for emotional survival as the infant's detachment during early loss experiences. It is necessary because the intense feelings are often all an individual can bear. Interacting with well-meaning friends and relatives can quickly become too much for an already overloaded emotional circuit. Since the loss involves a loss of that part of the self which was invested in the lost person or object, the self is damaged by the loss. One of the concomitants of loss is a temporary withdrawal from others, as if to protect ourselves from further emotional damage.

It is also necessary to shut out the world momentarily so that the pains of grief can be fully experienced and lived through with clarity. Bereaved persons sometimes fear (and with some justification) that the rest of the world will take away the feelings and memories that are all they have left of the lost person or object. Holding on to the feelings of grief is a way of holding on to the lost object. At least initially, it is important to respect the need to shut out the world lest it take away the last remnant of what has been lost.

A refusal to do the work of grieving distorts or aborts the process, because it means not letting oneself withdraw, making a premature demand on oneself to return to contact with the world. Like the person who tries to do too much too soon after surgery, and thus slows the recovery process, the griever who prematurely forces himself or herself back into contact with others is refusing to do some of the subtle work of grieving. Since reentry into the social world is supported by much of our society, and withdrawal is not, social pressure often inhibits this aspect of the work of grieving.

If withdrawal continues indefinitely, however, the process of grieving stops even if the feelings of grief remain. Obviously, one needs to move beyond such a preoccupation in the long run. But that is most likely to occur if it is possible to live through the self-centeredness of grief rather than trying to overcome it. Those who care may unwittingly compound the problem if they cannot be comfortable with the withdrawal. The detachment of a griever may feel to helpers like an unwillingness to be loved or helped.

This necessary detachment can become a theological problem for those who regard any form of self-orientation as a manifestation of sin. C. S. Lewis wrote: "The notes have been about myself, about H., and about God in that order. The order and the proportions, precisely what they ought not to have been."[33] Lewis implies that preoccupation with self for grieving persons is theologically unacceptable. Such a conviction often prompts religiously oriented people to put narrow limits on the time and emotional extent of grief. But being temporarily self-oriented is a necessary part of grieving, necessary for emotional survival. Without going through such a period, the grieving person cuts herself or himself off from the possibility of a fully relational life later. Temporary detachment and turning inward are a part of healing and cannot be viewed as contrary to the purposes of God.

6. Grieving Never Wholly Ends

> Others because you did not keep
> That deep-sworn vow have been friends of mine;
> Yet always when I look death in the face,

When I clamber to the heights of sleep,
Or when I grow excited with wine,
Suddenly I meet your face.[34]

These lines from the pen of William Butler Yeats express the theme of unending grief. The depth of attachments made throughout life is usually greater than we know, and therefore grief is often more intense than we had anticipated. The image, the memory of dreams and things and persons lost, never completely disappears from our minds. What was once a painful wound will become, with successful grieving, a poignant and sometimes pleasant memory, but not all the longing will completely disappear.

If it is true that grieving never ends, then it is also possible to suggest that there is no such thing as divorce. People may choose not to live together anymore, and may get a legal divorce, remarry, and be happy in their new marriages; but it is not possible to eliminate all memories or care or emotional investment in one's former partner.[35] Working with people through a divorce is most appropriately understood as grief work. The goals of grieving are as applicable at the end of a marriage as at the end of a life. When a second marriage occurs, moreover, it is important to pay attention to the lingering grief present for all involved.

To grieve properly is not to forget the lost object entirely, but to let that object or person "go" sufficiently to make new attachments and new investments in life. A lost loved one really does live on in memory, and that memory will color our lives from that point onward, but it need not and should not dominate our living. Proper grieving makes new attachments possible while living with old memories.

THE GOALS OF GRIEVING

Grieving is a process in which the deep feelings aroused by the loss are acknowledged and relatively fully expressed. It should be possible for the grieving person to discover and to express the pain, anger, guilt, and other feelings that are the common consequences of loss. To express these feelings also requires that they be heard and responded to by others. Crying out one's pain may be largely done alone, but some of that crying needs to be heard and responded to by others who care. Withholding or denying one's feelings will almost inevitably block a person suffering from loss from finding the relief and growth that come with what Granger Westberg has called "good grief."

Grieving is a process in which our attachments to the lost person or object are not entirely given up, but are sufficiently altered to permit the grieving person to admit the reality of the loss and then to live without constant reference to it. It is not necessary or even possible to clean away all memories, but it is important to prevent the loss from being the point around which we build our future lives. "But When Life Tumbles In, What Then?" Arthur John Gossip's sermon preached just after the death of his wife, contains these lines: "Many poets have told us of Lethe, the river of forgetfulness. But Dante, in his journeyings, came on another, the Eunoë, to taste the sunny waters of which is to have recalled all the gladsome and glorious and perfect things one has ever experienced. Eunoë runs beside the track all through the valley of the shadow; and a wise soul will often kneel, and lift a handful of its waters to his thirsty lips and . . . thank God for the splendour he has known."[36]

In successful grieving, the mourner gradually becomes able to make attachments and investments in other persons and things once again. All grievers must recoil from life for a while, but healthy grieving enables us in the long run to reattach ourselves to the world and to persons with whom we can have deep and satisfying relationships.

Finally, for the person of faith, *grieving is a process in which a belief system, significantly challenged or altered by loss, is restored.* When someone we love goes away from us, our perception of God is changed and sometimes severely disturbed. When we lose what we value, we wonder about God's providential care. Even when one's confidence in God is a source of strength in grief, it is still necessary to gain a new understanding of God in the face of the apparent senselessness of loss. The closer to us the lost person was, the more our thinking is influenced. When his friend Charles Williams died, C. S. Lewis remarked that it was not his idea of Williams that changed, but his idea of death. It was a statement of calm assurance about God's care. But that calm assurance was shattered when Lewis' *wife* died. Experience of loss and pains of grief tamper with our visions of God. We must eventually rediscover God as One who suffers with us.

IMPEDIMENTS TO GRIEVING

Not all grief-stricken people find themselves able to work their way through the thicket. To let go of a deep attachment, and, later, to permit oneself to make new attachments is possible only when the emotions strongly associated with loss can be felt and expressed. The principal impediments to grieving are mainly problems in allowing oneself to feel and to express deep feelings.

1. INTOLERANCE TO PAIN

There are people who cannot allow feelings of pain and sadness to come to conscious awareness, in grief or at any other time. Although they can acknowledge intellectually that a loss has taken place and that they are bereaved, they cannot allow themselves to feel the pain. They are making use of a psychological defense called *isolation*. There is probably no human being who has never used isolation as a defense against unwelcome experience. Such a mechanism slows down the process of normal grieving. (But the pain will usually express itself in some indirect way, because repressed feelings invariably return.)

2. NEED FOR CONTROL

Not allowing oneself to *feel* feelings is different from the inability to *express* them. Our culture regularly instills in us the notion that to show one's emotions is childish or neurotic. To admit one's grief verbally, much less to show it in one's face or body, is often taken as a sign of loss of self-control. This need for control is a serious impediment to successful resolution of grief.

Such a need to control oneself is given a variety of labels in American society. It is sometimes thought of as simply avoiding self-pity, as though all expression of feeling is evidence only of feeling sorry for oneself. For some, there is a fear that "if I begin crying, I might never be able to stop." This fear usually reflects a larger lack of impulse control. By whatever name, the need to stifle the expression of feelings is learned early and is deeply instilled in many of us. It is common for families to have unspoken—and therefore especially powerful—rules against the open expression of one feeling or another, and such rules clearly limit grieving.

3. LACK OF EXTERNAL ENCOURAGEMENT

In order to make room for medical technology, many hospitals have eliminated the family rooms or waiting rooms which once provided private space to begin grieving. The impulse in medical and nursing personnel to inhibit the expression of feelings by chemical means is very strong; powerful tranquilizers are in many cases routinely given to persons in acute grief situations, and these drugs are a serious impediment to grieving.

The bereaved are isolated socially; widows in particular are ruthlessly hatcheted from invitation lists. Traditional patterns of allowing time to grieve do not seem to fit within modern social structures. There is irony here; people are on the one hand expected to be back on the job shortly after the funeral is over, just when their pains of grief are often felt most keenly; but the same people who expect grieving individuals to return to work are unlikely to include them in social invitations.

Even the language we use about grief has, in many cases, a negative connotation. No one really wants to *fall apart* or *go to pieces* or *come apart at the seams*. It may be said—it often is—that Mrs. So-and-So finally *broke down* at the funeral and wept *uncontrollably*. Such language reflects fundamentally negative attitudes about grieving, while not expressing feelings (*"She held up so well"*) is described more positively.

In small social units, particularly families, one person may be permitted, even nominated, to express feelings fully, while other persons are forbidden to do so. Persons designated as "the responsible ones" in the family are counted on to take charge in times of stress, and thus the family unconsciously but effectively prohibits them from doing the work of grieving. Since the responsible ones must make the arrangements for the funeral and telephone all the family members and give support to the "weaker" ones, they have no time to grieve. Grieving, for such persons, comes later, and is quite often laced with anger at other family members for "not letting me grieve." In a kind of mirror image of such a phenomenon, a family may unconsciously appoint one or more "grievers," persons whose emotionality is supposed to be open, rich, and full. Because they are so good at expressing feelings, others in the family don't need to grieve.

The inability of a family to respond openly and constructively to loss has long-term consequences. Psychiatrist Norman Paul has found that when a family develops rigid patterns of interaction for handling intense emotions, it is usually because of unresolved (and stored up) grief somewhere in the family's history. The original loss may have occurred two generations before, yet the family's style is permeated with varying degrees of denial and of tactics to ward off losses and disappointments. The family develops what Paul calls "fixed family equilibrium."[37] Major changes are resisted. A family's inability to grieve is transmitted across the generations until the pain is too great and someone breaks the silence.

The consideration of impediments is a reminder that the work of grieving, like grief itself, will vary. The uniqueness of grieving is determined by our individual personalities and by patterns established by the culture. Who we are affects how we grieve. We learn such behavior first in our families. How a family responds to loss of any kind provides the experience for learning how to grieve. In some families, if you are sad, you go out to the barn or up to your room and close the door; it is not permitted to be sad in public. A family's intent to shape the expression of grief is likely to be consistent with the rest of the patterns established to keep things in emotional balance.

Although how people express their grief will vary, grieving should occur even in response to seemingly insignificant loss. Emotions are better expressed than repressed. That is generally true in life but particularly true in grief. The delay of grieving, like any delay in the expression of intense emotions, means that what is not expressed is "stored." Abnormality in grief is usually the result of insufficient grieving.

THEOLOGICAL COMMENT

The church has not always provided a place for people to grieve. Its liturgies have excluded most of the lament psalms. Christian theology, largely under Greek influence in the postapostolic era, promoted moderation in everything including grief. In our own day popular piety has led people to question the faith of those who grieve "too much." Scriptures have been interpreted to discourage grieving because of the promises of eternity with God. The following passage is often used to support this position: "We wish you not to remain in ignorance, brothers, about those who sleep in death; you should not grieve like the rest of men, who have no hope" (I Thess. 4:13, NEB). The deceased is better off with God. It is only selfishness or the absence of hope that makes us grieve.

It is occasionally argued that the I Thessalonians passage instructs Christians not to grieve at all. If we have hope in the resurrection of Jesus Christ, then we have no business feeling sad or hurt when someone we love dies. Our focus should be only on the resurrection; and, if we do experience grief or allow ourselves to feel the sadness, hurt, anger, and other emotions of grief, it is to be taken as a sign that our faith is deficient.

That position by no means reflects John Calvin's judgment on the passage. Calvin is plain and direct, and seems to wonder why anyone should see a problem with the passage. "In this passage," he writes, "[Paul] meant simply to restrain excessive grief. . . . He does not forbid us altogether to mourn, but requires moderation in our mourning." Later, Calvin writes: "Let the grief of the pious be mixed with consolation."[38] It is typical of Calvin to favor moderation over excess. But it is also characteristic to find him advocating attention to, and expression of, one's emotions.

There is nothing in the passage that offers an unambiguous clue to Paul's intent.[39] It would appear that the contrast is not between grieving and not grieving but between grieving with the hope of the resurrection before (and underneath) us and grieving as pagans did. There is repeated evidence in the book of Acts that the early church grieved the deaths of its members and friends bitterly, and similar evidence in the Gospels that Jesus himself grieved over losses from the personal (Lazarus) to the communal (Jerusalem). It is in fact an emotionally disturbed or frankly abnormal human being who does not or cannot feel deep sadness after suffering a major loss.

But the way in which Christians grieve should not be the way others grieve. The approach of the faithful to God quite properly includes deep and bitter lamentation. To bewail one's losses, and even to reproach God with them, is a stance that receives powerful support not only from the psalms but from the experience of the prophets, Jeremiah in particular.

Our roots in the Hebrew tradition, with the full support of the Old Testament as well as the New, testify to the appropriateness, indeed the necessity, of raising an angry clamor when struck with loss. Our baptismal vocation calls us to be full, whole persons, which means experiencing the full range of feelings naturally arising out of loss. The refusal to grieve openly and actively is essentially an atheistic stance, for it denies that we have a relationship with a God who covenants with us.[40]

People who have *no* hope, however, must manage their grief differently and sometimes in ways that foster pathology. The Stoic denies loss, attempts to freeze time, and remains turned inward, inaccessible to those who love and care for him or her. The Stoic argument is that losing self-control is losing one's basic stance toward life. Since by definition grief is irrational and often uncontrollable, not grieving becomes a sign of Stoic faithfulness.

Not so for the Christian. We are more free to grieve precisely because our faith is grounded in the promise of a Presence from whom we cannot be separated. It is God's presence, embodied in Christ and continued in the church, that provides a shelter from the fear of abandonment. The testimony both of the Bible and of the history of the Christian faith is that those who have a living relationship with a living God are willing and able to argue with God, cajole God, scream out their anger and pain at God. They can do that because for them God *is* a living person. The hallowed presence of the One who is the ground of hope sustains them through painful and sometimes terrifying loss. The hope that nothing will separate us from the love of God is the hope that endures; it is the hope that encourages us to bring our angry, clamoring, hurt, guilty selves to the throne of grace. Because of that hope, we are free to grieve more rather than less. It is hope that makes grieving possible.

PART III

PASTORAL
RESPONSES
TO THOSE
WHO GRIEVE

6
The Personal Ministry of Caring

Although grieving is by its very nature a lonely task, the resolution of grief requires the presence of other persons. The notion that time heals the wounds of grief is only partially true; time alone is never enough to heal the ravages of loss. Full release from the hold that emotions of any kind have on us depends on their being heard. Grieving is in part an interpersonal process, lonely though it may be.

This chapter is for helpers of those who mourn. We intend to provide a framework for assisting people to live with and through the pains of loss. There are times when grieving does not get done because friends, relatives, pastors, or counselors are unable to respond with empathy to the expressed pain. Impediments to grieving exist within potential helpers as well as within the grief-stricken person. We are therefore concerned about expanding the ability of helping persons to respond to grieving individuals.

The Christian community is the primary context for this consideration. Neighborhoods, social organizations, and work associations also attend to grief in significant ways, but it is in the parish church that major losses are publicly spoken about and ritualized. Congregations are still places that can organize themselves to care for those who grieve.

In the church, care for mourners is undergirded by the confidence that the future is secure in the promise of God.

> When Janet Olsen called to tell the pastor that her husband, Bryan, had died suddenly at work, she seemed surprisingly calm. She had already prepared a list of people to call and things to do. Efforts by the pastor—and, later, by family and friends—to assist her in preparations for the funeral were courteously rebuffed. She appreciated the offers of help, but insisted that Bryan would have wanted her to make all the arrangements. Janet understood herself as a responsible person. It was a shock to everyone when, eight months later, Janet angrily turned on her family. "I had no time to grieve when Bryan died," she said, "because I was saddled with so many things to do!" Her grief was complicated by her anger at family and friends.
>
> When his wife, Betty, died after a lingering illness, Bill Tyndale seemed at a loss to know what to do. The simplest decisions were overwhelming. Deciding what the children should wear or what to serve at the buffet required gigantic effort. Bill was relieved when some people from his church volunteered to prepare meals for a few days and to help with the children. It was a long time before he regained his customary efficiency.
>
> A hospital chaplain found Karla Wade in a utility room among mops and brooms. Karla's young daughter had died suddenly, though not unexpectedly, while Karla was out of the child's room, where she had slept every night for three weeks. Karla was racked with convulsive sobbing when the chaplain found her. From time to time she would hit her head against the wall and then bury it in her arms again. She would not be consoled. By the time her husband arrived she had been subdued by massive sedation. Her husband decided on the funeral home, agreed to

an autopsy, and then took Karla away from "all the memories here."

Janet Olson presents the most troubling problem for those who try to help grief-stricken people. She had long ago been "nominated and elected" by her family to be its responsible member, and she couldn't resign. Those who have been so designated will have a thousand reasons why they must make all the phone calls or plan all the meals. For Janet it was unthinkable that others should do "her" tasks. After all, everyone expected her to take responsibility.

Such a response to loss creates two particular difficulties. In the first place, one must respect the patterns built over the years in a family such as Janet Olson's. To challenge such patterns head on at a time of acute grief conveys a sharp disrespect for the different ways in which people handle crises. At the same time, one must be aware that those patterns are likely to have disruptive consequences for the family and its members. The other difficulty is that those who insist on being responsible through a time of early acute grief usually need considerable help after all the relatives have gone home and there is no one to cook for and be responsible for.

In Bill Tyndale's situation, Bill himself was overwhelmed. Intervention was necessary, and he welcomed it. He was immobilized by the intensity of his emotions and unable to function in his normally efficient way. He needed people to take charge of his life, to decide and provide, since he was temporarily incapable of doing so. Action had to be the central helping response. But this can mean that it is all to easy to intervene, to order someone else's life, and in the long run to foster an unhealthy dependency. Bill Tyndale took advantage of willing helpers to order his life until he married again eight months later. Yet it might be equally accurate to say that helpers took advantage of him. Fostering inappropriate dependency to meet the helper's needs is one of the subtler ways of abusing the vulnerability of grief-stricken people.

Bill Tyndale and Janet Olson illustrate almost precisely opposite ways of coping with loss. Neither overdependence nor overresponsibility encourages successful grieving. Those designated as responsible are too busy or active to back off long enough to feel the pain. Those overwhelmed by their grief find grieving too much hard work. Most of us are neither as immobilized as Bill nor as responsible as Janet, and can be more easily helped.

Karla Wade's grief was so intense that it overwhelmed those who tried to help. They were uncomfortable until sedation diminished the intensity of her feelings. She finally went home without any further protest against the absurdity of her daugher's death. Karla was further isolated by those who came to help. They made efforts to "manage" her emotions, but those efforts had the opposite effect; the ministrations were as intolerable as her feelings. But the need to manage is strong. Norman Paul observes that people generally have a strong aversion to letting themselves in for the grief, terror, and helplessness of others. "Before a person can empathize with someone who has those feelings, he must have been able to accept their existence in himself."[41] The reluctance of Karla's helpers to enter into the world of her grief was directly related to their inability to identify and accept their own pain. The critical question becomes not "What can I say to her?" but "How much of this can I hear?" Can we tolerate another's grief enough to allow it to reverberate within ourselves?

Emotional work implies, just as does physical work, the expenditure of energy against resistance. The work of grieving is intended to accomplish several goals: admitting the reality of the loss, creating a cherishable memory, beginning to make new investments and attachments, and reconstructing a faith significantly altered by loss. Accomplishing these goals requires intentional work as well as caring relationships.

MODES OF HELPING

In any attempt to do the work of grieving, we are likely to need four things, each of which may be provided by a particular mode of caring on the part of helpers. First, the griever often needs relief from the expectations of others, time and space to grieve. We have called the mode of caring which provides such relief *intervention*. The second need is for recognition and rehearsal of one's feelings, which calls for *support*. The third need is remembering, which is tied to the task of creating a cherishable memory. Here the resistance is often strongest, and the mode of caring most appropriate is usually *insistent encouragement*. Finally, we need to put ourselves back together, to reintegrate. *Reintegration* also implies reestablishing relationships and returning to significant communities. Here the helping behavior most appropriate is *conversation about significant themes*, and, sometimes, *gentle confrontation*.

For those who care, deciding which need is predominant and which mode of caring is most appropriate is sometimes a delicate task. Lengthy discussions about the nature of God in response to the question "Why did God let her die?" are appropriate and useful at a considerably later point in the process; in a time of acute grief early after a loss, such responses are useless if not destructive. In those early hours and days, the question is an expression of rage rather than an attempt to reexamine one's faith. On the other hand, the interventions helpful and necessary in early grief may foster or perpetuate an unhealthy dependence later on in the process.

1. INTERVENTION AND RELIEF

Every potential helper needs to be prepared to practice effective intervention. ("Intervention" literally means "coming between" someone and their problems, that is, taking over.) In practical terms, that means stepping in, taking over, and managing someone else's affairs temporarily, and stepping out again when the need has passed. If a helper steps in momentarily to take over, it is because those who have suffered an important loss are temporarily disabled.

We have said that numbness or emotional shutdown is the first response to major loss. With it comes a more pervasive paralysis. Usually well organized people such as Bill Tyndale become incapable of ordinary functioning. Even familiar tasks loom larger than usual.

The decisions precipitated by major losses are almost never easy to make. Bill Tyndale had no choice but to decide what dress his wife would wear in her casket; Karla Wade was too distraught, and so had to wait for her husband to choose a funeral director and agree to an autopsy. In losses of less magnitude, a milder paralysis is often visible. The loss of a treasured possession or an election or a valued friend may prompt us to postpone momentarily any decisions we can.

We therefore regard intervention as the most effective initial helping response. We understand it as any act that seeks to help people with their grieving by assisting them to handle ordinary tasks and responsibilities. In many cases, it means doing for people tasks which they would in almost any other circumstances do for themselves. This kind of action makes time and space for people to begin to do the work of grieving. It presumes that the helping person will take initiative or in some other way act on behalf of the bereaved person.

This is often simply common wisdom. Neighborhood groups and work groups, as well as churches, often demonstrate the capacity to mobilize responses to the needs of an individual or a family experiencing crisis. When people have experienced serious loss of some kind, it is generally regarded as acceptable to take responsibility for them in ways that at any other time would not be appropriate.

What is needed most of all soon after traumatic loss is time and space. Some cultural traditions have ritualized bereavement in ways that ensure time for grieving. We have mentioned the Jewish tradition of "sitting shiva" as a way of being related to a caring community; it is also a way of ensuring uninterrupted time to live through the pains of loss. Rather than being kept busy and distracted, grieving individuals should have as little as possible expected of them so that they have time and emotional freedom to experience the loss and feel the pain. Intervention to protect that time and offer that freedom usually shortens the period of intense grieving.

The Practicalities of Intervention: Doing Routine Tasks

Those who try to help mourners often become involved in so-called emergency feelings: feelings that *everything* is of world-shaking urgency. The feelings are partly true but mostly mistaken. Intervention often begins simply by assisting people to determine which decisions have priority, and which ones can be delayed, which tasks must be done by the primary grievers and which could be done by others. Each family will have its own set of priorities and rules; helpers must honor such family patterns, even when they are far from the helpers' own preferred patterns.

It may be a major dilemma for the family and for helpers to decide who must call which relatives when a death occurs. Some grievers may choose to make all the calls themselves in order to avoid hard feelings. Others may "give away" the most painful calls for fear they would not be able to continue a painful conversation. Even the ways in which we get in touch with friends or relatives may facilitate or postpone the grieving process.

> Margaret's husband had been sick for more than two years, and was hospitalized the last four months of his life. After her husband's death, Margaret asked the pastor to call her son, who was in the armed services. The pastor wisely suggested that the son would rather hear of his father's death from his mother. After an hour of angry and tearful resistance, she resolved to call her son. The pastor's reluctance to take over this particular task was in the interest of aiding Margaret's grieving, painful though the telephone call was.

Every act of intervention needs to be examined in the light of its effect on the process of grieving. Keeping a grieving person busy is really keeping a busy person from grieving. Other activity, such as Margaret's call to her son, should be encouraged, because it prompts the expression of grief by pointing to the reality of the loss.

Just managing the daily schedule may be more than grieving persons can handle. The "casserole brigade" is not just a warm, neighborly thing; it is an ongoing resource for intervention in times of crisis. Both the husband who assumes more than his ordinary share of household duties because his wife's father has died and the co-worker at the office who quietly assumes an extra amount of work when his friend's marriage is breaking up are acting on the recognition that an individual in crisis needs relief from ordinary tasks. Intervention is the mode of care that provides for this need.

The initial pastoral visit after a death has occurred requires particular sensitivity. Few pastors seek involvement in the intensity of grief, though they know it is their pastoral task; one way to avoid coming face-to-face with feelings is to be involved with the details of the funeral service. Some planning cannot be avoided, but it is important to keep the focus *on* the loss, not *away* from it. Selecting hymns and pallbearers and special music may become the occasion for thinking about the person who has died. It is a way of initiating the process of reminiscing that is central to effective grieving.

Preplanning is one way to avoid some of the decisions that become difficult to make in the midst of grief. Battling over plans may simply become another means of avoidance. But if the disposition of the body and the nature of the funeral can be agreed to in advance by the primary family, there will be more time for grieving.

Yet preplanning done without the agreement of the primary family may become an impediment rather than an asset. We respect those persons who wish to leave arrangements for services and rituals after their deaths. But the fact remains that *what we do at death we do for the sake of those who survive,* and therefore their desires should be given preference over the desires of the deceased. Rituals after death are for the sake of those who mourn.

The Practicalities of Intervention: Advocacy

Especially just after a loss, people who grieve need to be protected from those who would take advantage of their vulnerability, or who act out of a need to have the grief-stricken person live up to some imagined norm of behavior. Our society places an extremely high value on the avoidance of pain, to the point of preoccupation. In any society where a promise of fast, *fast*, FAST relief is an effective advertisement for a common pain-relieving drug, there will be those who will try to get the grief-stricken person to blot out his or her own experiencing.

But those who would dull the pain are at least acting out of some interest in the griever's welfare. Not all "helping" persons have an individual's best interests at heart. The most delicate form of intervention, often requiring sensitivity and assertiveness at the same time, is advocacy when one recognizes the possibility of abuse of a grief-stricken person. Such a matter as selecting a casket may require the presence of an advocate. Financial "advisers" looking for quick gain are eager to catch a grieving person unawares. Being an advocate is a way to create a safe time and space in which mourners can grieve.

Mourners need to be protected from themselves as much as from anyone else. In *Widow*, Lynn Caine records some very foolish financial decisions made in the initial emotional confusion after her husband's death.[42] No one can protect those who grieve from every possible bad decision or even from doing some crazy things. But the principle remains: mourners should be encouraged to postpone as many decisions as they can, not only to avoid some imprudent choices but also to make time for the work of grieving.

The Practicalities of Intervention: Treading Softly

Care always has boundaries that shift from situation to situation. It is usually assumed, for example, that potential helpers have the right to take over another person's life almost completely if that person is on the verge of suicide. But the impulse to take over must be kept within boundaries even in that situation; and the crisis of grief is not the same as a potential suicide. The impulse to take over completely is mistaken, as is the reluctance to intervene at all.

> Marlys Trundle effectively organized her entire household, but the organization depended on her presence. Then she died. The family was grateful when a neighbor volunteered to help out on the day after the accident. She did the wash, cooked the meals, and organized the visitation of friends and neighbors. Unfortunately, she presumed to do more than was appropriate. In an awkward moment, the neighbor had to be asked not to help so much.

The Trundles' neighbor violated appropriate boundaries, perhaps prompted by her need to be needed. Her activity diminished grieving rather than enhancing it; she protected the family from experiencing some of the pain which they actually needed to undergo. Intervention should be understood as an interim mode of care necessary only because grief is at first intense and bewildering.

2. SUPPORT FOR THE RECOGNITION AND REHEARSAL OF FEELINGS

Providing support for those who grieve is the second helping response to traumatic loss. Being supportive includes some aspects common to all caring: simply standing by as a listening presence comfortable with silence; bearing with individuals in their pain and confusion; responding encouragingly when strong feelings are expressed; and lending strength to people when they need an emotional "prop." Each component requires willingness to suspend or suppress the impulse toward premature comfort as a way of warding off pain. One must be able to listen without judging, hear without retreating, evoke without forcing, and understand without condescending.

The relationship established by being with someone in grief provides safety in which individuals are free to grieve without fear of abandonment or condemnation. Although it is not possible through our presence to eliminate the lonely work of grieving, we can at least eliminate the isolation that intensifies grief.

At best, pastoral work in grief builds on a relationship established before the loss occurs. Mutual trust and respect already exist. Even so, one cannot presume on what has gone before when caring for those who grieve. Whatever the previous relationship, a particular emotional connection needs to be established at the point of loss, to guarantee a strong and accepting presence. This is especially true when the loss involves divorce, suicide, or some other factor that may carry with it a load of shame.

Serious loss often calls into question the faith relationship of the bereaved, which usually needs reexamination and reintegration over a period of time. A pastor is not only the representative of the faith community but also the recipient of a significant and not entirely consistent transference. At the best of times, people project on their pastor their fears of judgment, their anger at God, and many other feelings. In moments of severe stress, the tendency to misperceive the pastor is even stronger.

A Listening Presence

Grief expressed is not grief heard unless someone is listening. Our being is validated in being heard. Standing by others at a time of loss means first of all to listen to them, to attend to their anguish, and to be present to them. We listen in order to stand in grief with another pilgrim, to transcend the barriers that isolate us from one another, to make the connections that diminish loneliness. We do not simply listen in order to know what to say. If that were so, then speaking would be more important than listening. To give one's whole attention to another is itself a gracious act.

In order to listen, it is essential to be comfortable with silence. As with any human situation, silence in grief has several meanings. In some cases, there simply are no words to express the pain. At other times, the silence is a consequence of numbness. The loss is sometimes so terrifying that ordinary patterns of speech are impeded. For still others, silence masks a caldron of rage unacceptable to the one experiencing it. One needs to be comfortable enough with silence to let it be without asking why it is there. Our own silent presence may become a source of strength if it grows out of a profound respect for the tragedy of loss and the horror of human suffering.

When listening to people grieve, we do not need to feel that we must answer their "why" questions. The "why" is an expression of rage as often as not. We can also be reasonably sure that listening is not concerned with the accumulation of information beyond hearing the details of the loss. If people repeat the same story about the last meeting with the lost person or give a plethora of medical and legal details, it means that for the moment they are stuck at a particular point in their grieving. The helper's focus must be (and can be) on the person telling the story, not on the story.

Empathy

Our first response to a grieving person is likely to be sympathetic. We begin by saying how sorry we are about another's loss. This is usually the message on the stan-dardized sympathy cards available in stores. Sympathy is of course not inappropriate; but it is not an acceptable substitute for empathy as a helping response. It is too subjective. Empathy involves getting outside of our own feelings enough to attend to another's experience, to feel another's anguish as distinct from our own even when it resembles our own. Empathy requires us to hear and receive what another human being is feeling and saying.

It is a crucial response because it links understanding with acceptance. Grieving individuals will often harshly judge their feelings as selfish, bad, crazy, or unchristian. Passing judgment on a feeling makes little more sense than passing judgment on Pikes Peak because it is in Colorado rather than in Montana. It is simply there. It is important that the puzzling and wild emotions of grief be heard and accepted so that people will be able to live through the loss.

Empathy requires both objectivity and imagination. Those who are inclined to see the world primarily through their own experience are limited to being helpful in situations in which they can readily identify themselves. Because grief is unique to each individual experiencing it, imagination is essential. It is neither possible nor desirable to depend on identification with one's own experience. We need to cultivate the capacity to imagine what someone might feel who has lost a spouse, a child, a breast, a job, or a dream. Our capacity to imagine another person's grief is cultivated through an examination of the losses common to life. In that sense, we always have the chance to learn how to be helpers of those who grieve.

Lending Strength

Emptiness, a dominant characteristic in the emotional reaction to loss, arises from the fact that all loss in some way depletes the self. Those who develop and maintain only a very small amount of autonomy in significant relationships find the crisis actually life-threatening when those relationships are severed. For some grieving persons, borrowing strength is necessary for emotional survival and even biological survival because too much of their self was linked to the lost person.

Ideally, lending strength is merely a temporary means of support. The capacity for autonomous functioning is, for most people, only momentarily impaired by the trauma of loss. The helping person needs to be someone strong enough to lean on, able to endure the intensity of grief and the depth of another person's needs.

Temporary or long-lasting, the need for support often makes grief-stricken people feel as though the slightest wind could topple them. Lending strength at such a point can mean merely giving someone permission to be dependent, trusting that such dependency is neither abnormal nor permanent.

> When Cynthia's husband died, her emptiness was devastating. After some months, she sought counsel-

ing; the counselor quickly became the new male source of strength, fantasied lover, dependable friend, and pastor. He could never do enough, be available enough, or give enough support to fill all the empty places. Her grieving became an overly long process in part because she did not wish to lose her counselor.

In fact, the helping person is seldom able to do enough to fill the emptiness created by the loss. For the sake of the helper's survival and the griever's growth and recovery, it is necessary to set limits on the extent and length of dependency one will allow. If the pastor or other helper needs to be needed, he or she may begin or continue to offer support inappropriately.

Limits need to be built in at the beginning, but support must not end with jarring abruptness. In many cases, support stops the moment the funeral is over. Pastors may not continue the kind of attention they demonstrate within the first few days. Once filled with guests and funeral preparations, the house is now suddenly silent and empty. A similar pattern occurs when a child leaves for camp or college or to get married. The emptiness is most keenly felt after the best-known and most usual systems of support have already diminished. The abrupt termination of support in turn creates its own grief, which then hinders the grieving process.

The Danger of Premature Comfort

Some responses to grieving persons may look support-ive but be unhelpful and unsupportive in the long run. For example, the direct giving of comfort is not essentially supportive, except for the kind of comfort that consists in touching, holding, and "crooning phrases" such as "Yes, yes," and "There, there." Comfort that strays far from these simple acts usually comes from our wanting to take the hurt away or to give reassurance that the pain will subside and disappear. So we seek to console by making promises that things will be better, that time heals all wounds, that God will take the pain away, or that things will get better on their own "if you don't make it worse by crying." (We find it difficult if not impossible to imagine a situation of genuine loss or sadness in which crying makes anything worse.) Under the guise of consolation, helpers may promise more than they can deliver and more than is necessary.

Premature comfort is in the last analysis no comfort at all because it closes off the painful but necessary process of living through grief. It is not helpful to promise that the pain will go away, even when it is true. We can usually promise, however, not to abandon people to the loneliness of grief. The promise of presence is, in the long run, the comfort that sustains.

Religious resources have all too often been used to provide premature comfort; they then clog the process of grieving. C. S. Lewis is pointed in his criticism: "Talk to me about the truth of religion and I'll listen gladly. . . . But don't come talking to me about the consolation of religion or I shall suspect that you don't understand."[43]

Assurances that the deceased is with God may set aside our anxiety about the future of someone we love, but they do not diminish our sense of loss. "For those who love life, immortality is no consolation in death," writes Simone de Beauvoir.[44] We agree.

The same dynamics are at work in all kinds of loss. It is some consolation to know that the daughter whom you miss terribly is having a wonderful time at college, but that does not fill her empty room. Premature comfort involves a refusal to understand grief and a denial of the self. What enables us to endure the pangs of grief is the experience of being heard and understood.

The "rush to meaning" is a variant of premature comfort. By this phrase we mean the inclination to answer why questions with a ready interpretation of the intentions of God or the mysteries of life. An all too quick explanation is a way to abort the process. For some religious people it seems to be more important to defend God than to attend to the needs of those who grieve.

Answering why questions makes of grieving an unhelpful intellectual exercise. Early in grief it is best to assume that why questions are expressions of anger and confusion. At the same time, the validity of the question should be acknowledged by an assurance that the question will be considered later in the grieving process.

In the journals of Frank and Letty Norbridge, a couple in their mid-forties, we find instances of helpful and unhelpful caring applied to the same loss situation. The Norbridges had been writing journals for about three years when their house caught fire while they were at the movies. Their baby-sitter and two of their four children were killed in the fire. Their journal entries over the next weeks and months reflect their responses not only to their multiple losses but also to various attempts to help them.

> (*Letty's journal, nine days after the fire*) Mrs. Nemerov stopped by today. I have begun to call her Mrs. Nembutal. I am ashamed of that, but I probably won't stop doing it. She is so eager to make us stop hurting. Today she quoted Paul: "All things work together for good for them that love God." It astounds me that she can't see that right now that's precisely what I cannot bear to hear. Timmy dead, Donita dead, and Beth Elton dead; and ALL THINGS WORK TOGETHER FOR GOOD? My soul cries out that they do not, they do not, they do not.

> (*Frank's journal, six weeks after the fire*) A strange thing happened today. I was standing and talking with Pastor Markham, and unaccountably began to cry. It was the pastor who saw the tears on my cheeks; I was unaware I was crying. He said some-

thing, and *then* I became aware of the tears. I was embarrassed and I began to apologize. And then Ed said something that hit me like a ton of bricks.

"Frank, if you can't cry, wail, scream, shout, and holler, there's something amiss with your faith or your theology or both."

"What?" I asked.

"Stifling your crying, even for Letty's sake, means that you're hiding what you really think and feel from God. What kind of theology is it if you can't yell at God? Whatever it is, it isn't a living relationship with God."

It was an hour before I was able to say that Pastor Markham was right. Why hadn't I seen it before? Why has my theology been so distorted that I felt I had to be polite to God?

The use of religious resources should first bring to expression the pain that is felt. Reading a psalm of lament is comforting even if it evokes tears, precisely because it validates a person's grief. Simply knowing that another faithful human being has experienced terror and rage helps to transcend the isolation that grief produces. This kind of ministry is faithful both to Scripture and to the theological theme of opening oneself unashamedly to God in faith.

INTERVENTION AND SUPPORT: SOME PROBLEMS

Even when the reality of loss is experienced in a way that evokes the expression of grief, it is not always easy to sustain that process long enough for the pain to be lived through to some resolution. Many factors, including fatigue, combine to make this the case. Grieving is difficult to sustain over an extended period, simply because it is hard work.

The absence of a supportive network is another factor limiting the work of grieving. Full awareness of the reality of loss often begins only after friends and relatives have resumed their normal routine and are busying themselves with other activities. Grieving persons often need help the most when friends and relatives are no longer readily available. Pastoral work at a time of loss is often needed to fill that gap.

> The Canton family lost their twenty-year-old son in an automobile accident. Grace, the young man's mother, allowed herself one month to grieve. As soon as her self-allotted time was past, all her life was resumed as before. The other children in the family saw mother's example. Now, some years later, Grace's married daughter Dorothy Thayer sets definite limits on how long she will allow her husband and children to be sad. Feelings in the Thayer family are often squelched before they have been sufficiently lived through. Grace Canton's legacy to her daughter includes a troubled marriage in which Dorothy's husband is significantly withdrawn from his wife. A major portion of that difficulty comes from Dorothy's having learned all too well a lesson about limited grieving from her mother, Grace.

American society tends to enforce an invisible limit to the expression of any intense emotional experience. "Enough is enough," someone may say, signaling that in that person's eyes it is time to stop crying and get on with living. Sometimes we impose limits on ourselves, because we have learned that it is "better" to internalize the hurt rather than to lose control and allow ourselves to be vulnerable. Isolation is the result; it is, in fact, the price we pay for appearing strong at all costs.

3. INSISTENT ENCOURAGEMENT: THE NEED TO REMEMBER

Literature on grief and grieving almost universally agrees that one major goal of grieving is to gain emotional release from the attachment to the lost person or object, but how is that emancipation to be achieved? There is a significant answer to this question: one gains emotional release from what is lost by actively making it a memory. Reminiscing or remembering with another person is the principal means by which we build such a memory, which in turn helps us gain needed emotional distance from the past. Planning for the future is also clearly linked to freedom from emotional involvement with the past. The work of grieving is therefore best understood as an alternation between remembering and hoping.

Initiating Remembering

The invitation to reminisce can begin with preparations for the funeral. There are unavoidable questions about the significant events of a life that make up an obituary. Ordinarily, these memories come easily at the time of death. The stories that extended families so often tell each other at funeral gatherings begin the process of making a person's life into a cherished memory. Such social gatherings are natural times for storytelling, socially accepted occasions for the convergence of tears and laughter. The sharing of past events also reaffirms and reinforces the family's boundaries.

Remembering can be a painful process; it is not always easily begun. The helping person may need to insist on remembering, an insistence that may be experienced as confrontation. When people are particularly vulnerable, the memory may indeed be too painful, and intervention and support are what is needed. However, there comes a time when gentle prodding is appropriate. To insist that the griever create memories and keep them bright rather than shut them away particularizes the memory of what was lost. It is the most effective way of diminishing the emotional investment in the lost object or person.

The shift from reality to memory is difficult for many people. "I just don't want to cry anymore." "I am tired of being sad." Working on a memory is like creating an internal emotional scrapbook. It is painful because it involves a flat admission that a loss has occurred. It is painful because it brings to awareness the complicated composite of emotions connected with the lost person. But there is no other way through grief. It is remembering that creates and sustains a memory. We need to nudge grievers, kindly but firmly, to acknowledge the reality of loss and to remember the person or the thing that has been lost.

Although this process of remembering may begin naturally around the funeral, the need for persistence is most likely to begin after the initial grief has ended. Memories become more difficult to share as the finality of loss is realized more clearly and the supportive community has withdrawn. The emergence of ambivalent memories may also make it more difficult to talk about the past. Pastoral initiative with those who grieve therefore takes on much added importance in the weeks following the funeral.

Enhancing Remembering

At significant holidays or anniversaries the absence of a loved one is particularly keenly felt because a familiar part of the ritual is missing. Christmas is not the same without Dad's presents wrapped in brown paper bags. What is Thanksgiving if Grandma does not cook the turkey? Wedding anniversaries are often painful even after the divorce is final. It is still an anniversary but with a different meaning. It can sometimes be a less obvious anniversary or holiday that evokes the painful memory. An outsider may not always know which holidays or anniversaries have particular significance. It is therefore important for helping persons to be alert to any number of major milestones that are occasions for reminiscing. One pastor, sensitive to such issues, wrote to a family on an occasion which he correctly thought might be significant.

Dear Wilma and family:
I did not know Duane, so I can only go by what people have told me of him. . . . I know he was a man of faith, a man of strong conviction. . . .

I wish I could have known him. It was two years ago today that he died. You and your family have sensed in different ways what he meant, how you miss him, and how that has been resolved.

May the strong grace of God be with you this day. . . .

Making an actual scrapbook is another way of enhancing the process of remembering. Joyce Phipps's husband died of a heart attack at a comparatively early age; they had children ages five and three. "We started a memory book in which we wrote an account of the things we had done with daddy. . . . It would prevent any quick forgetting, especially on the part of the three-year-old. It occupied a tremendous amount of time and it allowed a genuine participation on the part of the children. They could feel that the memory book was theirs and that their memories were as important as mine. Together we organized photographs, pasted them into the album, and composed anecdotes to be written beside the photos."[45]

Building a cherishable memory is equally necessary in divorce situations. Too often grown children are faced with the prospect of reconstructing a portion of their history because a mother or father refused to talk about a divorced spouse. Keeping such historical facts secret in a family is invariably destructive; it prevents remembering from healing the grief, and fosters fantasy at the expense of reality.

Some Problems in Remembering

Reminiscing is often resisted, because people in grief are sometimes stuck in "replaying" the moment of death or in re-creating the last significant encounter with the lost person. They continue to redirect any effort toward fostering reminiscing back to that last meeting. In a sense, limiting remembering to that last moment is a way of denying the reality of the loss; it thereby precludes the necessary healing.

A second barrier to remembering occurs when the lost person is prematurely canonized. We have already noted that such insistence on the lost one's perfection is frequently a signal of buried anger. (The presence of negative memories does make the process of remembering more complex.) In the grief that accompanies a move to a new location, it is easy to romanticize the community left behind in ways that exclude certain memories. It is not surprising that people who romanticize the last place where they lived have a hard time adjusting to new surroundings.

Grief occasioned by divorce can lead to an opposite problem. In order to keep alive the resentment that legitimates the divorce, positive memories may be excluded altogether. The one who holds tight to the posture of victim can only remember what is negative or painful about the marriage in order to preserve the myth of having been victimized. Such selective remembering also precludes the possibility of forgiveness that can bring healing to those memories.

> Megan McDonnell went to a pastoral counselor for help in learning to manage her two sons (seven and ten) after her divorce from Jerry. For more than six months, Megan's labels for her former husband were bitter: psychopath, liar, cruel. One day, the counselor (who had never seen Jerry) asked Megan if she had any pictures of him. At first, Megan said that she had destroyed every evidence of Jerry's existence. Then, reluctantly, she remembered that they had made an album of a vacation taken when Megan was pregnant with their first son, but she claimed to have lost the album. The following week, however, it turned up. A

laughing Megan, showing obvious signs of pregnancy, was clinging tightly in every picture to a huge, muscular Jerry. "You must have thought that Jerry was strong and dependable in those days," remarked the counselor. "Oh, he was, he always was." "It must be difficult," suggested the counselor, "to hold in your mind an image of a strong, dependable psychopathic bully." Megan began to laugh, and laughed until she began to cry. Bringing the two images together, seeing Jerry as a man with strengths as well as weaknesses, and still realizing that the divorce was a painful but probably correct solution to the problems of the relationship, helped Megan to begin to become whole.

A third sign that remembering is being resisted is the persistent use of the present tense when referring to what has been lost. Immediately after traumatic loss, there is understandable confusion about verb tenses, because time itself is out of joint. The moments immediately after a loss are not occasions for grammatical purity, but a sentence such as "Carl is a good husband" when Carl has been dead for eighteen months suggests that Carl is being held as a present reality rather than a cherished memory. An occasional reminder that the past tense is the appropriate verb form when referring to someone who has died is usually all that is needed.

The impulse to hold on to what is lost by holding on to significant associations with him or her is understandable early in grief. To hang on to signs of continuity is not necessarily a sign of pathological grieving. Indeed, precipitous removal of all reminders of the lost person before grief has been lived through can be an equally problematic sign of denial. Possessions or mementos are signs of continuity and useful symbols for building a memory. But if the room where she slept is left unchanged indefinitely, or if his clothes still hang in the closet ready for wearing, then we may be seeing an attempt to bypass the reality of loss. It is difficult to create a memory of someone whose return is expected.

It may therefore be a significant help to insist on disposing of his golf clubs, or sorting pictures after a divorce. Such insistence is somewhat confrontive, but carrying out these and similar tasks is as necessary as it is difficult. It is part of a process by which people gain emotional freedom from the continuing claims of the departed person.

Thanksgiving makes remembering possible; so, in another sense, does remembering make thanksgiving possible. The fundamental connection between the two is symbolized in the old Eucharistic prayer: "Remembering, therefore, his salutary precept, his life-giving Passion and Death, his glorious Resurrection and Ascension, and the promise of his coming again, we give thanks to Thee, Lord God Almighty, not as we ought but as we are able." When remembering leads to thanksgiving, then memories become cherished. By contrast, a feeling of being short-changed makes remembering, for those who grieve, the occasion for added bitterness. Such difficulties are most common when the loss is perceived as taking place "too early," leaving hopes unfulfilled. The capacity for gratitude makes it possible to bring closure to a life or a relationship, however long or short.

There will be grief situations in which remembering is resisted because the past is too painful, and other times when our efforts to help people build a cherishable memory will be thwarted by the conviction that there is little for which to be thankful. At its best, the expression of gratitude is a recognition of finitude. It involves the confidence that God does not condemn incompleteness, because it was God who determined life to be finite.

4. Reintegration

Gratitude makes remembering possible; remembering makes hoping possible. Remembering and hoping are inextricably bound together. The future is opened to new relationships and new experiences to the degree that the past has been made a memory. Reintegration as a mode of care is an expression of hope.

The final goal of living through grief is to restore a self depleted by loss, and to be able to resume previously significant relationships and activities, and to establish new patterns of living that take into account the loss that has occurred. It also includes rediscovering meaning in one's life and reforming one's view of God, since major losses often alter our understanding of God.

When the pains have largely been experienced, expressed, and understood; when the supportive community has gathered around one; when one has been able to let loved ones or loved objects or shattered dreams become a memory; then it may be appropriate to consider the why questions that were, earlier, more an expression of rage than anything else. Now those questions become a part of attempting to reconstruct meaning and reestablish relationships.

The Depletion of Self and Inner Restoration

The loneliness and emptiness of grief are the outward signs that one's sense of identity or well-being is more dependent on relationships than we generally realize. At times, this dependence may be close enough to the surface that the dread of being abandoned by someone we depend on for sustenance and identity will create a life-style of anticipatory grieving, but the full pain of the loss comes when the loss actually occurs.

All losses have the power to deplete one's sense of self: a job layoff, a Dear John from a lover, significant change in the department where one works. The death of a parent may hasten, for middle-aged sons and daughters, the discovery of autonomy, and force a recognition of finitude.[46] The death of a spouse often precipitates a crisis of self-sufficiency; the senseless death of a child is more likely to provoke a crisis of meaning; and if one's sense of self was significantly related to the lost person or object, there will be a crisis of self-depletion.

Such a crisis may lead to significant personal growth or to paralysis. If someone says, "I feel that three quarters of me is gone," there may not be enough self left to build a future. Those who have dependable personal support are more likely to "regrow" a sense of self.

Ironically, some losses convey to those left behind a freedom of which they cannot take advantage, because the self is damaged. To realize that one's growth in autonomy or creative freedom has been made possible by death or divorce is sometimes more than a person wants to face; the guilt is too great.

> Cynthia's restoration after Ralph's death took place slowly. She began to be able to use some of her creative gifts. Her letters to her therapist slacked off. Many years later, she wrote in a Christmas letter:
> I am braver.
> I am wiser.
> I am stronger.
> I am healthier in mind and heart.
> I am growing to love life and myself.
> But sometimes, when I decide I no longer need help, I get scared.

The restoration of self is often not unlike the concept of becoming "weller than well," Dr. Karl Menninger's phrase for becoming healthier than one was before one got sick in the first place Helping such a process to take place requires caution, for lending strength, no matter how appropriate at a particular time, may lead to becoming a replacement for the lost person.

The work of inner restoration consists largely in helping the griever to discover and foster her or his own internal resources. Those who care need to set and keep clear limits to their availability. Even when those limits may be experienced by the grieving person as indifference, they are necessary both for the growth of the griever and the survival of the carer. But the carer must understand the griever's reluctance to accept her or his own strength. A major loss causes changes in one's sense of self, and these changes are themselves experienced as a further (intrapsychic) loss.

Reintegration and Significant Community

Reintegration also has a social, interpersonal dimension. Those near a mourner often avoid contact; it feels awkward, and is connected with the stirring up of our own intense feelings. We don't know what to say. C. S. Lewis' image of the griever as leper is not at all surprising. The choice for grievers seems to be: either cover over the grief and resume your life as if nothing has changed, or, if you must feel the pain, do so in complete isolation.

Returning to association with friends and relatives is not easy for us or for them, because memories are evoked by the renewed contact. Beginning new relationships may take even longer, because opening a new relationship involves a confession that the loss was real. Inviting a friend going through a divorce to a meeting of Parents Without Partners is likely to be resisted until the reality of the divorce is acknowledged.

The ministry of reintegration into community may involve gentle nudging. Some people are relatively quick to resume old relationships as a natural consequence of seeking and using support. Others are slower to return, sometimes regarding their self-imposed isolation as a punishment for surviving. In order to help grievers, it is necessary to respect each individual's own timing, and at the same time to be willing to give an occasional gentle nudge.

> Maureen, a divorcée, found it difficult to resume social activities after her divorce. She and her husband had withdrawn from their primary circle of friends as it became less possible to contain their personal conflicts. After the divorce, the only social context where Maureen felt comfortable was with other divorced women. She was ashamed to face the people whose acceptance she desired. The feeling of being an outcast was confirmed by the reluctance of her friends to include her in their social gatherings. This pattern continued for months until her pastor insisted that Maureen fill in for a Sunday church school teacher who had to be absent for a weekend. His insistence was somewhat confrontive, but it served to reintegrate Maureen into meaningful community involvement.

The greatest encouragement toward resuming social interaction may come from people who have had similar experiences of loss. Identification may produce understanding. Programs such as widow-to-widow, THEOS (They Help Each Other Survive), and other social institutions for single persons may offer some useful support. Unfortunately, they also represent a segmenting of society which is itself a problem. To live in a segmented, segregated society means that one's primary social interaction is with those who have had similar experiences. The result is often divisive. The church needs to play a crucial role in breaking down the loss-induced barriers that keep widows off certain social lists and restrict retired persons to communities outside the mainstream of society. The church can be one place in society in which love and empathy do not demand identification, where pluralism is celebrated, and where grieving people are not isolated with "their own kind."

Reintegration and the Loss of Meaning

"Why did this happen to me?" is one of the most frequent questions asked in early grief. We have already suggested that this question should be seen initially as an expression of rage. As time passes, however, other internal needs spark similar questions. We want to know why tragedy occurs in order to tame, at least momentarily, the irrational forces that threaten to cripple our existence. Even when there are no simple answers, the why questions are useful because they keep the grieving alive. Eventually we need to find a way to incorporate the absurd into our understanding of life.

Having postponed answering such questions until some of the grieving has been lived through, helpers still need to avoid easy answers or facile interpretations. In the following conversation, Beth makes her own interpretation of her husband's stroke. The conversation took place with a pastor after an adult church school class. Beth, visiting, introduces herself to the pastor and tells him about her husband's illness.

> P: What are your feelings about the stroke now?
> B: I think God was trying to teach us a lesson.
> P: A lesson?
> B: I realize now we were not really focusing on God, but that we made money and financial security our God. We worked all those years to pay off the farm and put the kids through school, and we finally thought we were getting ahead when the stroke happened. Since the stroke, I've been thinking and I have come to the conclusion that God was trying to tell us we were to look to him for security and not to money. It's been hard, but I think we will be better off thinking about God more and money less.

Beth's way of making sense of her husband's stroke was to regard it as punishment from God. Rather than acknowledge that people have strokes because it is one kind of illness that people are capable of having, she interprets it as a harsh bit of divine pedagogy. A God who sends a stroke to teach such a lesson comes close to being C. S. Lewis' "cosmic sadist"; but this interpretation, though theologically deficient, was used by Beth to reorient her life and her faith. Her acceptance of the present for what it can be was informed by her gratitude that "we still have time together."

THEOLOGICAL COMMENT

An individual's faith may be sorely shaken by traumatic loss even though confidence in God may remain constant. The loss of someone or some valued object will inevitably raise theological questions about the meaning and purpose of life and the providence of God. For people of faith, suffering and loss eventually raise questions that cannot be ignored. Sometimes God seems very far away. At times of significant loss, facile statements about the goodness of finitude and the presence of God have a hollow ring.

It is most important to take the question of God seriously. Our theology or our world view is generally about as sturdy as a house of cards. One little wind is enough to blow it away. Significant loss is usually one of the winds that blow on the structure of our beliefs. The life of faith is an ongoing task of building and rebuilding. The process of reconstructing begins when the question of God is asked.

Those who grieve need first to be assured that God will endure our doubts and questions. Because we are confident that God will respond, we can live with deeply painful questions. Daniel J. Simundson has suggested that one role of the comforter is to protect sufferers from easy answers that come out of a narrow understanding of the

Bible or of Christian faith.[47] In the midst of the distress of loss it is comforting to remember that God suffers. It is equally important to demonstrate God's suffering love by *our* willingness to listen to suffering and grief, and not give in to the impulse to run from the pain, shut off the complaint, or respond too quickly with pious platitudes. We need to avoid the rush to meaning in any form, for living through grief requires an ability to tolerate unanswered questions.

If time is provided to live with the question and to live through the grief, it will be possible to develop a genuine reaffirmation of faith. In *A Grief Observed*, C. S. Lewis traces the process: "When I lay these questions before God, I get no answer. But a rather special sort of 'no answer.' It is not the locked door. It is more like a silent, certainly not uncompassionate, gaze. As though He shook His head not in refusal but waiving the question, like 'Peace, child; you don't understand.' "[48]

The recognition that God is present even in the questions of doubt and the rage of disbelief is often the key to reintegration. We rebuild our fragile theological house, taking into account the new questions that have arisen because of the pain of loss. Rebuilding is enhanced by the awareness that God suffers with us in the embodied presence of those who watch with us in grief.

It takes courage to accept suffering as a consequence of finitude without rejecting finitude as evil because of that suffering. To be human is to be finite and to suffer. The isolation that suffering creates is transformed by the assurance that the God who hung on the cross always suffers with us. It is he who enables us to suffer with one another.

7
Public Ministries
to Those Who Grieve

As a community gathers around those who have undergone serious loss, or as it huddles together under the impact of its own loss, two things usually happen. First, the community repeats certain rituals, most of them, though not all, drawn from its religious tradition. Secondly, the community usually "commissions" someone to speak publicly both for them and to them. Both practices usually involve an effort to weld the community together, to make some kind of sense out of the absurdity of life, to "make things make sense again." In Christian funerals, these two tasks are combined in one form, where the liturgy (ritual) and the sermon (public speaking) are one ceremony.

For the purposes of this chapter we are going to separate worship and preaching, examining each ministry separately. We will also discuss other kinds of rituals and public speaking which have to do with other experiences of loss in life.

WORSHIP

Rituals evolve in response to transition or change in order to help manage the powerful feelings aroused by the loss. (Change is always experienced as loss, even when it may also be experienced as gain.) The feelings may be "managed" by encouraging *ex*pression or *re*pression. In some Christian rituals frank recognition of mourning, sorrow, and grieving is not encouraged. In the Presbyterian *Worshipbook*, for example, one can see the downplaying of strong feelings of grief. The emphasis is on God's action that lifts us out of the distress of grief.

By contrast, the *Lutheran Book of Worship* (1978) elects to recognize, to permit, and to bless mourning and grief. The prayers in the service for the Burial of the Dead are frank in their recognition of pain and sadness. They express the theology that in such condition we can be lifted from it by God's consolation. The resurrection of Jesus Christ and the Christian's hope of sharing in that resurrection are strong themes in that Lutheran service. But it is assumed that casting one's sorrow on God and relying on God for solace and consolation is where one must begin.

Both perspectives need to be present in rituals of ending. Funerals, although the best-known rituals of ending, are not the only ones. Since the funeral is indeed the best-known such ritual, many of our examples in this chapter will be about them. All rituals of ending, including funerals, need to maintain the balance between remembering and hoping which we have identified previously. Worship at the time of loss needs to recognize the human condition of sorrow and distress while at the same time the presence of God is remembered and proclaimed.

Human beings use rituals at any point where significant change has taken place or is about to take place. Almost invariably, change is experienced as both loss and gain; most transitions are simultaneously the beginning of something and the end of something else. By and large, any particular ritual emphasizes one aspect of the transition and plays down the other. We can therefore conveniently divide rituals into two major categories: rituals of beginning and rituals of ending.

A wedding is essentially a ritual of beginning. Most of the focus is on the new life into which the couple is entering; there may or may not be a fleeting reference to the families being left behind as the couple forms a new family. Aside from bachelor parties, it is unlikely that there will be any reference at all to the sometimes painful fact that both bride and groom will be abandoning a particular life-style in favor of a different one.

Our culture also ritualizes endings; the retirement party is a well-known example. At such times attention is paid, with varying degrees of seriousness, to the fact that something else is also beginning. Religious groups could, if they chose to do so, ritualize divorce in a manner similar to that of the funeral or the retirement celebration. Some United Methodist churches appear to have already informally done so. Robert Farrar Capon, on the other hand, argues powerfully against ritualizing divorce, suggesting that the end of a marriage is a metaphysical impossibility.[49]

Both rituals of beginning and rituals of ending pay some attention to looking forward and looking backward. The emphasis in one direction or another is useful. But in every ritual of ending there are elements of beginning, and vice versa.

RITUALS OF ENDING

The funeral is primarily a ritual of ending. The elements of beginning in it are largely denoted by theological themes such as resurrection. Such elements should be clearly present but should never overshadow the ending elements to the point that the fundamental identity of the funeral is lost. As a theological theme, witness to the resurrection is obviously right. However, to emphasize it in a funeral at the expense of an emphasis on ending denies the nature of the event being symbolized by the ritual. What happens in such cases is seldom an emphasis either on beginnings or on endings, but a denial that there has been any transition at all. The use of theological themes or theological language to support denial works against the grieving process.[50]

The Funeral as Part of the Grieving Process

It is important that the ritual of ending not be seen as something separate, apart from the work of grieving. The nature of grief and grieving applies to the funeral as well as to other rituals of ending. Funerals should encourage and enhance expression of grief in a supportive community, as well as celebrate the promises of God in the midst of loss. Funerals should embody an alternation between remembering and hoping, themes that we have already identified as fundamental models of grieving. It may seem to go without saying that the funeral is part of the grieving process, but all too often rituals of ending have ignored or even discouraged grieving.

Sometimes the discouragement is fairly subtle. There may be little mention of the deceased, little specific reference to the immediate mourners. The liturgy and the preaching may focus on victory in ways which, while accurate reflections of God's promises, may at this time discourage the sadness necessary for successful grieving. For instance, the new Roman Catholic liturgy for the dead celebrates one's baptism as the garment of promise at the cost of neglecting the fact that we stand face-to-face with death. The theological assertion is accurate, but from a pastoral perspective the theological priority has been misplaced.

Rituals that acknowledge endings need to be frank and straightforward in order to enhance the process of grieving. If they are not, they will in the long run not perform the task of helping people to grieve. In the case of the funeral, this means a frank acknowledging of the reality of a person's death. Joseph Matthews tells how distressed he was by the pretense that nothing was really going on at his father's funeral, as if the service were to be some kind of meaningless ritual. He wanted to cry out: "Something *is* going on here! My father's death is going on here!"[51] The clear finality, without euphemisms, that a death is a death is most likely to help people get on with the work of grieving.

When the funeral is understood as a part of the grieving process, it is clear that it should enhance rather than impede the expression of grief. The open expression of feelings is to be encouraged rather than discouraged. People should be allowed to cry in church; more, the crying should be affirmed. The selection and use of religious language in the funeral should be governed by this need to facilitate the expression of grief.

Ritualizing Remembering

The enhancement of remembering is a significant part of the ritual of ending; it is the means by which the community begins to make the one lost a part of its collective memory. The funeral, or any other ritual of ending, is an ideal time for corporate, as well as individual, remembering. The problem, however, is that remembering sometimes turns into sentimentalizing. (Sentimentalization is essentially the exaltation of one emotional aspect of a memory at the expense of others.) Funeral eulogies which idealize the dead person limit the development of full and realistic memories of the person who has died.

This principle works equally well in other rituals of ending. At a recent retirement party there was a speech thanking the retiring woman for her contributions to the welfare of the company for which she had worked. One of the administrators reminded the retiree and the crowd that Sally had often made other employees angry by her insistence on using her own system of accounting for certain informal funds under her care; her system had caused considerable discomfort to those who had worked with her. After the party, one employee was heard saying to another: "You know, it would have been just plain hokum if Jack hadn't said that about Sally. One thing all of us will remember was the crazy way she handled the Emergency Fund. That needed saying, too." The process of grieving for the real Sally was enhanced.

Grieving is enhanced in a ritual of ending when the remembering tells the whole story. In order to avoid improper idealizing of individuals in death, many funeral services have ignored mention of the deceased altogether. In most instances, the memories that people bring to a ritual of ending will be mixed. The following remembrance of a man named Harold that was read at his funeral attempts to make mixed memories explicit.

> Harold will be missed in many places beyond the neighborhood and family. The 6:30 Mass at Mercy Hospital will need to get someone else to take up the collection. He will be missed by many recovered alcoholics who took their first step with Harold. It was his ministry; he would even leave a Gun Club dinner to answer a first step call. He was as dedicated to AA as he had been to drinking. . . . They say he was a mediocre euchre player even on his good nights—but he was always so delighted when the gang would gather. Someone has suggested that the smile he took to his grave was the same as the one he wore when he euchred Paul Miller. . . . There were many sides to Harold Nachtman. This is true for all of us, of course; Harold was just not very good at hiding his many sides. So we come to this place . . . to honor Harold and to support his family; to pray that God will be gracious with his faults; and to remember a man about whom everyone had at least a couple of things to say. We will all miss Harold, and we will all remember him.

Since a ritual of ending is a part of the grieving process, it should have within it the elements we have noted earlier:

frankness about the fact of an ending, encouragement of the expression of feeling, and enhancement of remembering. Since such rituals usually come quite early after a loss has occurred, it is appropriate that priority be given to expression more than to integration.

A Ritual of Ending Exists for the Mourners

If the funeral is understood as a part of the grieving process, then its primary focus is on the immediate family. It is first of all for them that the ritual exists. Whether the funeral is liturgically fixed or relatively free, it is important to take every opportunity to personalize the ritual for those who mourn. Friends who may not be family but were close to the deceased need also to be included as mourners. The presumed intimacy of family life often produces emotional ties more laden with meaning than those which develop outside the family, but this is not always the case. Some ties outside the family are deeply significant and need to be recognized as worthy of support for grieving.

Rituals of ending should provide a supportive context for those who mourn. They should be able to come away with the sense that they are members of a caring and supportive community. They may be so immured in their grief that their own aloneness is for the moment more powerful than the presence of others to give support, but at some level that presence is available to awareness. The supportive ministry of others cannot be casually dismissed because "she wouldn't know we were here, anyway." The funeral needs to be, whenever possible, an expression of communal solidarity.

The death of a particular individual may mark the close of an era in the community's life. The changing of one business establishment, perhaps the closing of the last bookstore, may be *the* mark of neighborhood change. When a newspaper drops a comic strip and replaces it with another, the standard practice is to advertise the new strip and to ignore the removed one, to treat it as if it had never existed at all. Such a practice is frequently a trigger which causes a subscriber to cancel a subscription. A change, no matter how small, may mean the end of an era.

When it is not possible to hold a community funeral, a memorial service or a memorial time within the context of regular Sunday worship is often appropriate. We recall a funeral attended by a large number of the deceased's out-of-town relatives, held at a time that suited their convenience, but when a very large number of his fellow church members were away. No memorial service was held in the church, and six months later people were still coming up to the widow to say that they had "just heard" about her husband's death. In many of these comments there appeared to be a certain disappointment and even resentment, as though the hurried funeral on a major holiday weekend had robbed them of the opportunity to grieve for themselves and with the family. Although it is difficult in many urban situations where people belong to a variety of groupings, communities need an opportunity to ritualize the loss of a significant member.

Consistency with Christian Theology and Values

A ritual of ending within a Christian community must be consistent with Christian values and traditions. Unfortunately, we are often under pressure to behave in ways inconsistent with those values. People spend lavish and unnecessary amounts of money in order to appease unresolved guilt in relation to their deceased loved ones. Expensive caskets and blankets of flowers do not cover the need for forgiveness which is finally the gift of God. Elaborate funerals are, moreover, instances of poor stewardship.

Funerals often seem designed to create or maintain an air of unreality contrary to Christian realism about death. In his essay, "The Time My Father Died," Joseph Matthews describes his strong reaction to the contrived nature of much that went on after the death of his father. Choosing a casket, Matthews and his family learned that prices varied widely. When they asked for the lowest priced casket, the funeral director at first refused to sell it to them, claiming that it was reserved for paupers. He also refused to bring it out where they could see it. After the family finally persuaded the mortician to let them see this "totally unacceptable" coffin, it turned out that it was a simple pine box of the kind used a century ago. Matthews erupts in rage about "the great concealment by means of plush caskets, white satin linings, soft cushions, head pillows, Sunday clothes, cosmetics, perfume, flowers, and guaranteed vaults. Empty of symbolic meaning, they serve but to deceive—to simulate life. . . . What vanity to denude death! All our pretenses about it only strengthen its power to destroy our lives. Death stripped of meaning and dignity becomes a demon. Not to embrace death as a part of our given life is finally not to embrace our life. . . . This is the power of unacknowledged death."[52]

Theological controversy continues to swirl about funerals. Cremation presents a problem to far fewer persons today than it did even a few years ago; but there are still individuals and groups that have trouble with it. Whether or not a church funeral can be held for a suicide is still a problem for some. There is also a question of parallel services being held by lodges, paramilitary groups, and quasi-religious groups. In some denominations a person may have a Christian funeral or a Masonic funeral, but not both.

It is no simple matter to affirm our faith in the resurrection in a society in which a wide variety of other themes and beliefs has found acceptance. At times, these other beliefs are set forth as though they represented Christian theology. The belief in individual survival which crept into Christianity some centuries after the apostolic era is popular enough to be found in the thinking of many persons and churches.

Making individual survival central, placing all one's hope in the "natural" immortality of the soul, is sub-Christian. It needs no Christ. It is a belief tied more to the doctrine of creation than that of redemption. The proclamation of the resurrection at death is about the nature of God more than about human survival. The promise of continuity in the face of the radical discontinuity of death is grounded in the dependability of God. In the midst of the funeral itself, it is important, though not easy, to maintain a faithful witness to the Gospel while at the same time paying attention to needs that will facilitate grieving.

SUMMARY: RITUALS OF ENDING

A ritual of ending is a part of the grieving process; therefore it should say seriously and realistically that an end has been reached, and should symbolize that end; encourage the expression of feelings related to that end; and enhance the remembering of what has been lost.

A ritual of ending exists for the sake of those who have undergone the loss; therefore their needs should supersede most other needs, but the existence of a larger community that shares in the loss should be recognized.

A ritual of ending within the Christian tradition should be consistent with that tradition; therefore such rituals need to be controlled by the standards of the Christian group in which they take place. In the case of death, they should celebrate the Christian hope of the resurrection. It is finally that hope which makes grieving possible.

It is clear that death is not the only kind of loss we face, not the only ending to which we have to pay attention. It would be enriching if in fact there were rituals of ending to mark the many other losses through which we must live. And if all major change contains elements both of beginning and of ending, it may be valuable to identify some of the endings that are present but unnoticed in other rituals.

THE ENDINGS IN BEGINNINGS

The old custom of giving away the bride at weddings is essentially sexist, reflecting the belief that a woman is her father's property to be given away. Yet the departure of the bride from her family of origin (and the departure of the groom from his) does symbolize the end of something, and is attached to the losses that members of both families feel—and rightly so—at a wedding. We have argued elsewhere that the crucial issue in launching a successful marriage is making a clear separation from one's family of origin.[53] To do so entails loss; it is entirely appropriate that such a loss be ritually marked in the wedding. Where the "giving of the bride" has traditionally stood it is well to have a ritual of farewell of both bride and groom from their respective families, with a clear and sharp emphasis on the necessity of taking emotional distance from one's family of origin.

Looked at in the light of what we have said about rituals of ending, such a ritual would clearly state that the dependence and obedience owed to the authorities in one's family of origin are now at an end. The biblical claim in Genesis and Matthew is essentially that one is no longer a member of one's family of origin. It could invite parents to engage in some remembering, and to state their own hopes for the future. It can make it possible for people to weep without embarrassment. People do all these things at weddings precisely because they are in fact emotionally and spiritually right. Sheldon Harnick's song in *Fiddler on the Roof*, "Sunrise, Sunset," does precisely what we prescribe: ritualizes the loss, allows for feelings, for remembering, for hoping.

For younger parents, the baptism of a child, particularly of the first child, contains within it elements of loss: loss of freedom, loss of an earlier life-style, along with the fear of being displaced. A baptism should take public note of the change and be frank about the relationship of change and loss. Such ritualizing has power to speak to a situation in which loss often goes relatively unnoticed.

Perhaps one of the most familiar yet seldom recognized cases of ending in beginnings is to be found in the ritual known as commencement. Commencement usually celebrates the culmination of much hard work, the beginnings of new freedom, entry into society at a new level. But also present is a great sense of pain and loss for many. There is an emptiness for some and an awkwardness to the farewells, as graduates stumble over words and make promises that cannot be kept.

Informally, some institutions have done rather well at symbolizing endings and creating the possibility for remembering and hoping. On the day before graduation, seniors in one college gathered to honor their classmates' exceptional achievements. Instead of meeting in an auditorium, they met outside, on a greensward around an old buried cannon. They smoked clay churchwarden pipes together, and, at the conclusion of the ceremony, broke the pipes on the cannon.

Another school, considerably smaller, organized a senior banquet at which the principal entertainment was the showing of a slide show of memories from earlier years, accompanied by tapes of Barbra Streisand singing "The Way We Were." The pictures were a mixture of funny and serious shots.

Most of the rituals of graduation exercises, however, are designed to emphasize the stability and continuity of the institution. In itself, there is nothing wrong with that. But such ceremonies seldom symbolize endings. The emphasis on continuity (supporting the institution) overshadows any emphasis on ending that would be more supportive of the graduates' needs and feelings.

MOURNING HIDDEN LOSSES

At the beginning of this book, we told the story of a church that was forced to relocate; in that story, the grief of the parishioners over the loss of the old building was managed, in part, by the replication in miniature of the sanctuary of the old church as a chapel of the church rebuilt in a new location. It is not likely that anyone consciously applied a careful understanding of loss and grief to that situation, even though what was finally done was an expression of the principles we are advocating here.

The story of the church's relocation is an example of an unconsciously helpful response; it may in other cases be possible to respond with conscious intent to help manage and foster a healthy grieving process. In many cases, the problem is to see the themes of loss and grief in what is going on. Perhaps the proper response will be personal and private; perhaps it will be public and ritualized. In either case, being attentive to the elements of loss whenever there is a change to be managed opens the possibilities of ministry.

When the Protestant Episcopal Church prepared a thoroughly revised *Book of Common Prayer*, many supporters of the change were concerned about ways in which it might be managed. Some were aware that many church members felt strongly that the revisions were not simply thorough, but radical. Others were so wedded to the new version that they denied that leaving the old *Book of Common Prayer* behind was going to be accompanied by a massive sense of loss.

In some dioceses, people found ways to say "good-by" to the old book. There were celebrations of its values, recognitions of its growing difficulties, remembrances of its words that had comforted people for more than four hundred years, and some laughter at its growing awkwardness in a linguistically changing society. These were

ways of ministering to the sense of loss felt very powerfully throughout the church. Even for those for whom the
new liturgy was a great gain, the loss of the old liturgy was
a great loss. To grieve that loss adequately was to prepare
more adequately for entry into a new phase of the church's
life.

Similar feelings have emerged on the part of a number of
Roman Catholics at the loss of the Mass in Latin. Responding more to their pain than to any historical or theological
warrant for the Latin Mass, some of them formed a
traditionalist movement, which holds to the Latin Mass.
The key issue was not divine ordinance of the Latin Mass;
few thought seriously that God had decreed the language
of the Mass to be Latin rather than a vernacular tongue.
The key issue was loss and intolerable discontinuity with
the past.

We have stressed throughout this volume that grief is an
appropriate response to significant loss of any kind. By
identifying rituals of ending, we have suggested in a
similar way that there are many loss experiences that need
to be ritualized. In a sense, the funeral remains the model
ritual, especially when it is structured around an alternation of remembering and hoping.

PREACHING

On Wednesday, June 8, 1966, a tornado ripped
through the city of Topeka, Kansas, leaving in its
wake almost twenty human deaths and millions of
dollars of property loss. Much more recently, the
town of Times Beach, Missouri, had to be evacuated
because dioxin, a deadly poison, had been found in
the ground. In a Midwestern city of 65,000, the major
industry, a maker of electrical parts for automobile
manufacturers, announced that it was moving to a
larger metropolitan center. Approximately 15 percent
of the employees would be given the option of

keeping their jobs and moving with the company to the "big city"; the other 85 percent of the employees would be "terminated with regret."

By now, such situations are familiar to readers of this book as losses, situations that will call for grieving, and for ministry to those caught up in them. Preaching is one aspect of that ministry. Some of the principles involved in developing rituals of ending and similar liturgies also need to be reflected in preaching. But preaching has its own special meaning and functions, and we shall examine those here.

MAINTENANCE OF REALISM

The first function of preaching in loss situations is to maintain for those who grieve a faithful contact with reality. That in turn requires attention to three issues intertwined with each other: the facts of loss, biblical realism about loss, and the theodicy problem. These three issues are so intertwined that it is difficult to separate them, but each can be discussed on its own.

The Facts of Loss

At first, this issue appears quite simple: preaching in loss situations needs to involve frank recognition of the loss. To some people, however, such frankness—even in situations not involving death—seems too brutal. After the Topeka tornado, a pastor remarked, in the first few minutes of his sermon on Sunday, June 12, that the tornado had torn a swath a half-mile wide through the city. A few complained that such dwelling on tragedy was unnecessarily unkind to those who had lost their homes. (No one who had lost their homes complained.)

Although in personal ministry we may temporarily accept the use of denial, it is not useful for the preaching ministry to foster the use of denial. The moments when denial is an expected response to the news of loss have passed by the time the preaching event occurs. In addition, the fostering of a community culture of denial is seldom if ever appropriate.

This means, among other things, that euphemisms should be carefully avoided. Words such as "died" and "death" and "dead" are far preferable to any of the euphemistic phrases such as "passed away" or "left us." Nor is it useful to gloss over the fact of loss in favor of a proclamation of hope. To preach hope before a loss is fully recognized and confronted is in fact to lose the power of hope. One cannot offer an answer before one knows the question. Preaching in loss situations needs, then, to identify the loss clearly without softening the consequent pain by avoidance and denial.

Biblical Realism About Loss

The biblical record makes it clear that loss is not unknown to even the most faithful of God's people, and that loss is not punishment nor a violation of the order of creation. The twelfth chapter of The Book of Jeremiah is one of many passages to make such assertions. The prophet has come to God with a set of scathing complaints, many of them involving Jeremiah's own sense of loss. Then comes the famous text (Jer. 12:5): "If you have run with the footmen and they have wearied you, how will you contend with men on horseback?" Here God promises Jeremiah that worse is still to come Similarly, Jesus promises his disciples that they will have tribulation, not that they will not. The same tribulation is reflected in Revelation 7, where the implication is that those who are singing songs of triumph around the throne have come through great tribulation rather than having skipped it. This will serve to remind us that trouble, loss, and grief are part of the "order of the day" for Christians and non-Christians alike.

When a minister is, through preaching, attempting to help people deal constructively with loss, this note of biblical realism needs to undergird the message. The opposite assertion, that "if only we have enough faith" God will not permit loss to befall us, is not only theologically unsound; it also leads the grieving person to wonder what is wrong with his or her faith.

The Theodicy Problem

But these biblical assertions bring us up against another problem. Eventually, all grieving persons who are believers—indeed, all believers—are confronted with a problem which, in the technical language of theology, is called the question of theodicy: how can a loving God permit pain and evil? The question can be put in many forms, some of them more theologically precise than others, but its basic thrust is always to highlight the difficult dynamic of God's power, God's love, and the pain in the world. Whether they have called it by this technical name or not, most serious Christians wrestle with the issue at one time or another, and some have found it the starting point of serious doubt about their faith.

We bring this issue up at this point primarily to say that it is precisely what the minister should *not* preach about at a time of loss, when grief is acute. The time of acute loss is, to be sure, a time when the theodicy question in some form is on the minds of those who mourn. But the question is raised at such a time and in such a form that preaching about it is the least useful way of dealing with it.

We do believe that sermons attempting to explore theodicy and related questions are an important part of overall ministry. Indeed, the groundwork for our ministry in particular cases of loss is a broader ministry of preaching, education, and pastoral care which does wrestle with difficult questions relating to pain and suffering [54] The place for that kind of preaching is not funerals, but in the general, ongoing ministry of the church.

There are in fact times when the issues of grief and grieving ought to be raised in the pulpit aside from preaching at the time of immediate loss. If the preaching ministry deals with grief only at a time of acute grief, and only with those who are suffering the immediate loss, opportunities for the church to frame and correct its beliefs are bypassed, to the detriment of the development of a lively theology.

With very few exceptions, grieving people do not need, nor can they use, a sermon about this difficult practical and doctrinal problem. Most such sermons tend to be a rehash of a paper written for a seminary professor, but that is not the real problem. The real problem is that sermons whose primary task is the clarification of doctrine are not a useful part of this particular ministry at this particular time.

PERMISSION TO FEEL

A second major function of preaching in loss situations is to give legitimacy to the feelings grieving persons have, about which they may feel uneasy or guilty. Persons in grief situations are usually thought to have a great many feelings; but such feelings are often experienced with great uneasiness. The sermon is often the most useful means of legitimizing those feelings in all their complexity.

> Not long ago a pastor died suddenly while on vacation. The congregation seemed very slow to go through the processes necessary to begin work on selecting a new pastor. Denominational officials were puzzled by the slowness. A few weeks later a guest preacher familiar with our principles preached for the congregation, using Psalm 137 as the basis for his preaching. His sermon suggested that the psalmist was both hurt and angry. It was filled with illustrations of faithful men and women screaming and

shaking their fists at God. Soon thereafter, the congregation moved to hire an interim pastor and to begin the search process for a permanent pastor. They had been angry with the pastor for dying, angry with God for having "taken" him, angry with the pastor's widow who had left town to begin her grieving process in her son's home several hundred miles away. The anger at the widow was particularly strong. The fantasy, of course, was that she, too, had deserted the congregation, yet they felt guilty for having such angry feelings directed toward a grieving widow. Giving them permission to feel their feelings, and letting them know that it was legitimate and even an act of faith to tell God directly that they were hurt and angry, helped not only to unlock expression of feelings but to release energy for necessary administrative work previously bottled up in an unfinished, indeed almost unbegun, pile of grief work.

Preaching in a time of loss is often found to "give permission" simply by identifying the hurt. Being able to put a label on something strange is usually a key to being able to manage it. The reason why certain feelings have not been felt is not that they have not been present, but that a standard set of defense mechanisms is brought into play to avoid conscious awareness of the feelings.

The identification by the preacher that "we shall not always feel this way, but this is how we feel now" has particular usefulness. It identifies real but unfamiliar feelings. The reestablishment of characteristic defenses should not be seen as some kind of blunder. In many cases, good pastoral care, either in person-to-person situations or from the pulpit, may consist in helping people to push away feelings that are difficult to manage. But such pushing away *is* a blunder if it takes place before the grief-stricken person has an opportunity to identify and understand the powerful feelings evoked by the loss. It often reflects the inaccurate judgment that "feelings are wrong," and may lead to the judgment on oneself that one behaved badly in a time of loss.

Many well-meaning friends and would-be helpers of persons who have undergone significant loss will attempt to extend comfort by saying, "You should not feel that way." That is likely to be one of the most emotionally destructive statements in the English language, and is certainly so at a time of loss. The emphasis needs to be on the fact that "you do feel that way, and for now you need to feel that way, but you will not always need to feel that way."

The sermon is a particularly valuable context in which to assure people that feelings are not wrong; it speaks to the community of people who share, at varying levels of intensity, in the loss. There is thus an opportunity to influence a community's response, though the preacher cannot always hope to persuade the entire group that feelings are permissible.

Proclamation of the Gospel

The proclamation of the gospel is common to all preaching. When we undertake a discussion of preaching as response to loss, the first question that arises is: What is the distinction between the gospel and mere optimism? The nature of Christian hope is such that it is quite different from optimism; but the nature of human nature is such that we often confuse the two.

Hope cannot be a bland, cheerful insistence that things will be all right soon. Such blandness and cheer, though countenanced and even encouraged by some forms of theology and psychology, is essentially unsatisfactory. It has earned hope a bad name among many serious thinkers, because it depends upon a weak grasp on reality. In many cases, our losses will be followed by no restoration of the specific person whom we have lost.

Nor is the gospel simply an invitation to expect that in a world to come our losses will be restored to us. The essential gospel promise is that we are never separated from the love of God. This does not mean that we should not hope to be reunited with those whom we have "loved long since, and lost awhile." But much of the gospel hope is realistic and this-worldly. It has to do with the ability to live joyfully in this world despite irretrievable loss. We reminded ourselves earlier that Jesus promises his disciples that they will have trouble in this world. The next line the Lord speaks is not an otherworldly line. We are to be of good cheer—not in a life to come but in this life—because Christ has overcome the world. This line speaks of hope that is connected with our recovery from grief and our ability to work through a process of grieving, sometimes in spite of the fact that what we have lost will not be returned to us. The hope is not specifically a hope of recovery.

The elderly widow whose fifty-year collection of photographs of her family and her marriage was blown away by the Topeka tornado has lost those pictures; they are gone; they will not return. Losses are losses; ends are ends; that is the context in which hope must operate. This is not to say that the gospel promises no restoration. The restoration it promises is a restoration to God's own self, a reattachment to the life God gives us. A quick and easy word that softens the reality of loss is not gospel; gospel is a loving, working word that promises our presence to each other and the presence of the Holy Spirit within that community of sharing. In that sense, there is always a mutuality to our hope.

The following is a portion of a sermon preached at a baccalaureate service which touches on the principles of preaching in loss situations we have identified.

> We are between adventures, and here we can celebrate our triumphs and lick our wounds a bit. The

celebration will be warm and good and fun, and we may find ourselves wishing it would last forever. But it won't. There is no treasure to be found here. The warm fire will dwindle to ashes. The company of celebrators will dissolve. The drinks will cease to flow. And so we must go. But if we go . . . ah, we may never see each other again. Never again *this* companionship. Never again *these* joys. Perhaps never again a pause for rest. . . . On my last adventure, I lost battles. I won battles. Some of my wounds will heal soon, some never. I have come to love some of my companions so dearly that I can hardly bear to leave them. I have been brave, and I have been a coward. I am not really sure I want any more adventures. But I see the King standing in the doorway, and he is saying, "Come!"

We have chosen this sermon excerpt precisely because it is not a funeral sermon, and yet must obey the same principles as a funeral sermon would have to follow. It is clear and forthright about the fact of loss. It deals openly and encouragingly with feelings. And it affirms that beyond this particular place of grief the hearers are called to relationships and tasks in Christ's world. At the same time, the resistance to moving on is taken into account. There is a focus on remembering, though little of that is visible in the sigment we have quoted. The needs of the mourners are attended to, the mourners here being the graduating students rather than the others who may have been present.

This particular commencement took place within a Christian context, and the baccalaureate sermon was based on God's call to Abram, who had settled comfortably in Haran, to move on to Canaan (Genesis 12). Moving on, whether out of Haran into Canaan, or out of school into new responsibility, involves both loss and gain, and capitalizing on the gain (realizing the promise) is more possible if one can mourn the loss.

PUBLIC MINISTRIES

Liturgy and preaching are to some extent separable categories, but any permanent separation of the two can be artificial and dangerous. To conclude this chapter, then, we return to a discussion of public ministries as a whole, including both the symbolic representations of liturgy and the verbal representations of preaching.

The special ceremonies that so often mark change points in life—dedications, commencements, funerals, baptisms, and the like—usually take place in connection with some form of loss. Often enough that loss is accompanied, and many times overshadowed, by a sense of gain. The dedication of a new building brings with it the joy of accomplishment and pleasure in the anticipated use of the new facility. But there will always be those who are aware of the loss that is taking place at the same time. A powerful version of this theme, by the way, is to be found in the third chapter of The Book of Ezra.

If we use the four categories of the ministry of pastoral care we suggested in the previous chapter, it would seem that the principal function of public ministries is supportive. There is little intervention, because in public ministries there are few aspects of mourners' lives to be taken over. Confrontation is appropriate somewhat later in the grieving process, and we do not usually expect to see it as a part of public ministry. The long-range integrative tasks do not at first seem to fit, either.

It is not only special occasions ritualizing change that call for ministries focused around loss. We do well to remember that the year-round liturgical and preaching ministries offer a variety of opportunities to engage in a ministry oriented toward the needs of those who are grieving, or to lift up for a congregation the elements of loss in an otherwise 'ordinary" event.

The baptism of the first child in particular is an appropriate moment to take note of the radical change in life-style a first baby demands from a couple.

Taking note of the changing neighborhood around a church not only permits the congregation to grieve the loss implied in neighborhood change but often sets the congregation free to reattach itself to new life in the neighborhood, and thus to minister more effectively as a congregation to its new surroundings.

In a congregation that pays careful attention to the liturgical year, such festivals as All Saints' Day (where loss and departure are a natural focus) as well as the whole scope of Lent, in which God's grief is so often an underlying theme, all offer opportunities to help members of the congregation to grieve openly and adequately.

It is fundamentally helpful for the pastor to learn to be alert to the ordinarily unrecognized elements of loss and grief in "routine" situations, and include them as a part of the church's public ministries.

8
Toward a Theology
for Grieving

The structure of this book is intended to follow roughly the sequence by which we experience and cope with loss and grief. Thus it is appropriate that we come now to a theological consideration of the place and meaning of grief in human life. Having begun with a statement of the problem of loss and its pervasiveness in human life, we then considered the origins and dynamics of grief and the characteristics of good caring. Each of these sections was informed implicitly and explicitly by a theological theme.

A SUMMARY OF THEOLOGICAL THEMES: FINITUDE, LOVE, AND HOPE

1. CREATION AND FINITUDE

Our understanding of the pervasiveness of loss is organized around the conviction that finitude is part of the creation which God regarded as good. Finitude, including the physical death of our flesh, is a necessary part of the orderliness of life. It is our inability to live with finitude that is the occasion for sin. That inability, ironically, plays a large part in putting us under the power of death. If we must organize our lives to deny the reality of finitude, then it is death rather than life which is the primary power in our lives. To regard finitude in general as good does not imply that particular instances of loss are good. The whole of creation, ordered by God to have beginnings and endings, has been so thoroughly disrupted by human sin, by our insistence on giving and withholding beginnings and endings, that the natural, God-given finitude in creation is destroyed or distorted beyond recognition. It will not be easy to claim finitude as a good; yet we affirm that it is so.

2. LOVE AND THE BREADTH OF GRIEF

The inevitability of grief and the appropriateness of grieving are consequences of human love for the world God has made. Because God has made us people of passion with needs for loving and being loved, it is understandable that we are sad when we lose what we have loved. In passing, we note that the passion and the will to love and be loved are part of the *imago Dei* in the sons and daughters of Adam and Eve. God is not passionless; God loves and suffers. The absence of love for people and for things is a mark of stinginess contrary to the extravagance of God's love intended to be mirrored in humankind. "'Tis better to have loved and lost than never to have loved at all." say Congreve the playwright and Tennyson the poet. We regard that as a theological statement, because loving is the human way of being. We have deliberately made no distinction between grief over the loss of people and grief over the loss of things. To insist that grief over the loss of things is of a lesser order is to separate history from creation. The loss of a snail darter or of the family farm or of a historical building are all significant losses for humankind, and indeed for the whole of creation marked by the interdependence of all things. The Christian's love for the whole of life is in response to God's extravagant love for the whole of creation.

3. CARING AND HOPE

Our understanding of care for those who grieve is largely undergirded by the conviction that Christian hope is a mutual act. In his *Images of Hope*, William Lynch suggests that we hope *with* as well as hope *for*.[55] The Christian hope sustaining those who grieve is an experience of mutuality as well as an anticipation of the future with God. About that future with God we can say very little except that God is faithful in death as in life. Meanwhile, we embody hope by our mutual love and support. Because time stops for those who grieve, it is particularly important that our care for them focus on the present. Hoping with those who grieve is an act of mutuality in the present that leaves the future with God.

Christian approaches to creation, to love, and to hope have informed our approach to loss and grief. Although they have been implicit in previous chapters, we are explicit about them here in order to identify the theological assumptions that have both preceded and flowed from our considerations of grief. Because creation is limited, and because we cannot live alone, to be human is to grieve.

A THEOLOGICAL EXAMINATION
OF THE CHOICE TO GRIEVE

In the Sermon on the Mount, Jesus says: "Blessed are those who mourn, for they shall be comforted" (Matt. 5:4). The original Greek translated here as "those who mourn," *hoi penthountes*, implies active lamenting: crying, wailing. A few modern versions retain this active sense: the Russian *plachushchie*, and, in a slightly different sense, the German *die da Leid tragen*. But many other contemporary translations reshape the active mourning into a passive state of feelings. Here, then, is a place where theological presuppositions have very likely influenced the translation of a word, the meaning of which, in the original language, falls clearly on the active side.[56]

The necessity for actively grieving losses is obvious. We may choose not to grieve, but inevitably we do so to our own detriment, if not to our emotional and spiritual peril.

We take the beatitude at face value: Those who mourn can be blessed because they can be comforted. It is difficult if not impossible to comfort someone who does not mourn. The beatitude embodies a human truth for all people and places: that the resolution of grief presupposes its expression. Those who bury their grief, put on a brave face for all the world to see, neither invite nor allow the kind of care that can bring comfort. Those who do mourn may be comforted.

But grieving is and must be optional even though the feeling response of grief is not. Theologically and pastorally, it is important to honor a person's freedom not to grieve. A fundamental principle of pastoral work is at stake here: respect for defenses. In nonclinical terms this principle means that we are not to violate a person's reluctance to grieve even when we know it would be better for that person to do so. We do not mean to retract anything we have said in this book by issuing this caution. Instead, we write to remind ourselves and all helpers that we dare not violate an individual's freedom even for the sake of that person's health.

The beatitude places sorrow-bearing at the center of Christian discipleship. On that matter there are no options. Those who claim Jesus as Lord bear the grief of others because they belong to a Lord who suffers and who in his suffering reveals God as one who suffers. The beatitude makes a telling demand on caregivers. We cannot turn from sorrow. We cannot ignore those who grieve. There is no need to seek suffering or to generate pain or suffering in order to share in the marks of Christ. There is more than enough suffering in the world for the Christian to bear for the sake of Christ.

"The disciple-community," suggests Dietrich Bonhoeffer, "does not shake off sorrow as though it were no concern of its own, but willingly bears it. And in this way they show how close are the bonds which bind them to the rest of humanity."[57] Bearing the griefs of others is not optional for the Christian who embodies Christ's compassion for the world. Our love for all humanity and for our particular neighbors compels us to stand beside them in their grief. Luther's translation of the Greek *pentheō* as *Leid tragen*, "carrying sorrow," suggests both bearing one another's burdens and open, active grieving.

The demand to bear the suffering of the world comes with a promise. Because Christians live in fellowship with the Crucified One, "they bear their sorrow in the strength of Him who bears them up, who bore the whole suffering of the world upon the cross."[58] From this perspective, the beatitude addresses an often forgotten issue. What of those who care for the grievers? What is the impact of their own work upon them? The beatitude contains a great promise. Sorrow cannot tire them or wear them down; it cannot embitter them or cause them to break down under the anguish of those who grieve, because they are comforted by the Crucified One.

We have suggested earlier that the Pauline line, "do not grieve as those who have no hope," is to be understood to mean that Christians are free to grieve more profoundly and deeply because they know that their life is grounded in God. In a similar way, Matt. 5:4 encourages us to bear sorrow fully and deeply with the assurance that we are empowered by the one who bears the world's suffering in his crucified body. In dynamic terms the meaning is straightforward: we can bear another's grief fully as long as it does not become our grief, but belongs to God who suffers with us.[59]

A THEOLOGICAL PERSPECTIVE ON
SUFFERING AND GRIEF

Loss and consequent grief are a part of life. Human beings cannot be understood as creatures outside the limitations of suffering and death. Sorrow is an inescapable dimension of the human. At a general level, the answer to the perennial question, Why do we suffer? is simple: we suffer because we are human. Because we are bound by the limits of birth and death, because all that we love is limited, because we are people for whom attachment to temporal things is inescapable, we suffer. Our task, as Tillich has suggested, is to accept and affirm suffering as a part of finitude and yet affirm finitude in spite of the suffering that accompanies it.[60]

Consider, in contrast to that picture of suffering in life, the widespread vision of a life without negativities in which happiness is a right. It is embodied in the "bronze dream" of bodies with a gorgeous tan, free from pimples and wrinkles and crooked teeth. The forces that hurt or deform or cripple are considered to be outside real life, accidental to it. Pain, boredom, loneliness, dread, rage, grief: none of these is "normal." From this perspective, crippling deformity and pain do not belong to human existence. So we hide the aged and deformed. We seek to remove signs of human imperfection in order to sustain our myth. The result is apathy: the illusion of painlessness, supported by the notion that Christ was born "in the beauty of the lilies." Apathy literally means the inability to suffer, and it produces a life-style that must avoid human relationships in order to avoid suffering.

Our problem is not insensitivity so much as impotence in the face of oversensitivity. We know and see more than we can bear. Behind the bronze dream lie accidents and dreadful meaningless pain and uncontrollable earthquakes and senseless crime and soil erosion and pulverizing technology, and then death. Our insistence on the pervasiveness of loss and grief in human life is in the interest of realism about human nature. It is a plea to know suffering as a way of overcoming the destructive power of apathy. In order to suppress the experience of suffering in human life it is necessary to muffle the passion for life and the strength and intensity of joy.

If it is human to suffer, then the principal theological question when we are confronted by loss and grief is not Why do we suffer? but Who suffers with us? Freedom from suffering is a blindness. The willingness to bear another's sorrow is the recognition of the reality of suffering in human life and the acceptance that the grieving person and his or her circumstances are normal. To be a follower of a crucified Lord is to be a bearer of sorrow. For that reason the Christian is always an alien in a world determined to deny death, to cover over loss and grief, and to ignore or stifle those who grieve. It is our ability to suffer with one another that modifies the loneliness of grief and eventually brings some closure to our sadness. The Christian's capacity to feel the pain of others transcends apathy and alienation. But in the last analysis it is the assurance that God suffers with us that is the rock on which we stand in all the turbulence of grief.

For some, this is a surprising, even radical, picture of God. Many people go through life with the expectation that God can and will eliminate our suffering. Such an expectation has led to endless frustration and anger at a supreme deity who seems either powerless or callous, and who at the very least has failed to maintain a world without blemish. The affirmation that God suffers with us shifts the focus from resolution to mutuality. Intellectual understanding of specific human suffering is impossible. There is no way to make sense out of the experience of parents whose firstborn is hydrocephalic, or out of the experience of older parents whose twenty-one-year-old son is senselessly murdered. Some human suffering is forever a part of the mystery of God. *But biblical Christianity has never promised that it would be any other way.*

Two things are essential: that we understand grief in relationship to community and that we be sure that God will not abandon us in our grief. Walter Brueggemann has wisely suggested that it is the covenant which provides the context for grief and loss, in which life is characterized by faithful hearing and speaking. It is in covenant community that we experience the bearing of sorrow. The purpose of the "lament forms" of the Bible was to "enable and require sufferers in the community to experience their suffering in a legitimate life-world. It is this form which enhances experience and brings it to articulation and also limits the experience of suffering, so that it can be received and coped with according to the perspectives, perceptions, and resources of the community."[61]

The question about God which grief raises is not God's power or goodness but God's faithfulness. Brueggemann notes that the form of lament in the covenant community makes it possible to address God directly. To address God directly even in anger is an act of confidence that one's sorrow and suffering have not driven God away. Loss and grief are real in human life and equally real in the presence of a faithful God. No amount of pain and suffering can separate us from the God who suffers with us. The life, death, and resurrection of Jesus affirm to us that God is not apathetic, but a faithful listener who suffers our pain with us.

The pastoral task is primarily concerned with keeping open communication between the grieving person and God. We do that best by our own listening to the cry of distress. Those who grieve are most likely to believe that God has heard their pain and has been touched by it if they experience the presence of those who are willing to suffer with them. Preaching the faithfulness of God, no matter how accurately and honestly, is for the grieving person a less effective way of carrying out such a witness.

ACTION IN THE FACE OF SUFFERING: A FURTHER QUESTION

Why is there suffering? is first and foremost a question that arises out of our pain and rage. It is a question that the pastoral carer does well not to try to answer, particularly in early grief, since the question is not even raised because the sufferer wants an answer. In fact, the sufferer can almost never accept any answer offered. It is almost as if the question is asked only so that those whose feelings are overwhelming may have something to which to say "No!"

Who suffers with us? is a question born out of our terror and isolation. It is the haunting plea not to be abandoned in the confusion of grief and sorrow. The covenant community is the enduring context in which to experience loss and grief so that we can endure.

There is a third question which leads to action: What are the causes of suffering and how can the conditions that produce suffering be modified or eliminated? For Dorothee Soelle, that is the first question. She is intent first of all to separate avoidable from unavoidable suffering. She affirms that God is not the cause of suffering, either to test or to train. When we look at suffering in concrete instances, there is no innocence. In her provocative book *Suffering*, Soelle sees no middle ground. You are either with the victim or the executioner. "That explanation of suffering which looks away from the victim and identifies itself with a righteousness that is supposed to stand behind the suffering has already taken a step in the direction of theological sadism, which wants to understand God as the torturer."[62]

It is not enough to recognize, as we have, the many ways in which loss and grief are a part of the human condition. Helping people to endure suffering which can be eliminated is neither kind nor just. The final action of grieving is ethical reevaluation. We have already suggested that some of the losses we experience in life are results of life-style rather than life cycle. It is the task of pastoral care and of social ethics to distinguish between avoidable and unavoidable suffering. The grief is essentially the same, however one understands the source of the suffering. But the ethical distinction is necessary in order that our suffering with those who grieve will eventuate in action to eliminate unnecessary suffering. Those who are most likely to work for that kind of justice are those who are suffering. Bearing sorrow is therefore not simply a pastoral necessity; it is an ethical obligation so that we do not lose the ability to perceive the suffering of others.

A CLOSING WORD

One final theological word is in order. Providence and finitude are the principal theological categories that undergird our approach to loss and grief. Our finitude is evidence of providence. It is God who has given us what we are and has set the limits to our existence. In middle age we become more conscious than ever before of that providence. The theology appropriate to a middle-aged person is a theology that recognizes plainly and with considerable joy the freedom that comes in knowing that whatever we do will not save us. Childhood and adolescence and young adulthood are all, almost by their very nature, deeply touched by works righteousness, as if we could, by using all our gifts, buy time and save ourselves and defer any thought of there being a limit.

Death completes our earthly sojourn. It is ultimate finitude. Only when a life has been rounded off by death are we able to set it in its own autonomy. It is finitude that makes completeness possible. Therein lies judgment. It is a sobering moment when a parent of middle-aged children dies, but the awareness of finitude is also a gracious moment. All our achievements are finite but so are our failures. Our lives are finally judged according to limited possibilities. We are free to live and love and learn in the confidence that the God who ordained the boundaries of life will accept our finite completeness.

Notes

1. Colin Murray Parkes, *Bereavement* (International Universities Press, 1972), p. 7.
2. Otto Rank, *The Trauma of Birth* (Robert Brunner, 1952).
3. Robert J. Lifton, *The Broken Connection* (Simon & Schuster, 1979), p. 62.
4. Margaret S. Mahler, *On Human Symbiosis and the Vicissitudes of Individuation* (International Universities Press, 1968). Biologists would be critical of Mahler's very idiosyncratic use of the word *symbiosis*, which for biologists has a highly specific meaning. Strictly speaking, symbiosis implies that both organisms joined in the symbiotic relationship are equally dependent on each other's presence for survival. It is clearly not the case, and clearly not Mahler's intention, to imply that the mother is as dependent upon the infant for survival as the infant is on the mother. The true biological parallel to the mother-infant relationship is not symbiosis; it is in fact closer to parasitism, but it is psychologically somewhat repellent to describe an infant as a parasite on its mother.
5. Ibid., p. 34.
6. Melanie Klein, *Our Adult World and Its Roots in Infancy* (London: Tavistock Publications, 1960).
7. Ibid.
8 John Bowlby, *The Making and Breaking of Affectional Bonds* (London: Tavistock Publications, 1979), p. 127. Ethology is the study of the development of social behavior and familylike relationships in nonhuman species. It is usually assumed that such studies can illumine our understanding of human social behavior. Each species has behavior peculiar to itself (species-

specific behavior) in matters such as feeding and mating, as well as others. Ethologists tend to argue that it is unlikely that such patterns are learned; instead, they suggest that species-specific patterns belong to the nature of the organism, and are imprinted in the species. It is possible to analyze a complex sequence of behavior such as courtship or nest-building, to isolate those features in the sequence which are inherited, and to discover the internal or external signals that activate or terminate such behaviors.

9. John Bowlby, *Attachment*, Attachment and Loss, Vol. 1 (Basic Books, 1969), p. 208. Attachment theory is a way of conceptualizing the propensity of human beings to make strong affectional bonds to particular others and of explaining the many forms of emotional distress and personality disturbance, including anxiety, anger, depression, and emotional detachment, to which separation and loss give rise. Also cf. Bowlby, *The Making and Breaking of Affectional Bonds*, p. 137.

10. Ibid., p. 63.

11. Theodore G. Tappert, trans. and ed., *Luther: Letters of Spiritual Counsel*, The Library of Christian Classics, Vol. 18 (Westminster Press, 1955), pp. 53–81.

12. Ernest Becker, *The Denial of Death* (Free Press, 1973).

13. John Hick, "Toward a Christian Theology of Death," in Gilbert Cope, ed., *Dying, Death, and Disposal* (London: S.P.C.K., 1970), pp. 22ff.

14. Erich Lindemann, *Beyond Grief* (Jason Aronson, 1979), pp. 61–64.

15. David K. Switzer, *The Dynamics of Grief* (Abingdon Press, 1970).

16. Sigmund Freud, "Mourning and Melancholia," in *Standard Edition*, Vol. 16, pp. 72ff. *The Diagnostic and Statistical Manual of Mental Disorders, Third Edition* (DSM-III) identifies grief reactions as phenomena that may come to the attention of professional mental health workers, and may require help; but grief reactions are specifically listed in a separate section of the manual devoted to phenomena that are not classified as mental illnesses.

17. Parkes, *Bereavements*, pp. 5–6.

18. Ibid., p. 173.

19. C. S. Lewis (writing under the pseudonym of N. W. Clerk), *A Grief Observed* (Seabury Press, 1961), p. 13. Future references to this book in these notes will be listed under Lewis rather than under Clerk.

20. In *The New York Times*, March 24, 1972.

21. Lily Pincus, *Death and the Family* (Vintage Books, 1976). This is a particularly good study of the relationship between patterns of marital interaction and the grief of widows.

22. Lynn Caine, *Widow* (William Morrow & Co., 1974), p. 97

23. Ibid., pp. 97–105.

24. Lewis, *A Grief Observed*, pp. 12–13.

25. Bowlby, *The Making and Breaking of Affectional Bonds.* For a more thorough discussion of this point of view, cf. John Bowlby, *Separation*, Attachment and Loss, Vol. 2 (Basic Books, 1973), pp. 3–32.

26. Lewis, *A Grief Observed*, pp. 25 and 27.

27. Walter Brueggemann, "From Hurt to Joy, from Death to Life," *Interpretation*, Vol. 28, pp. 3–19. Cf. also Donald Capps, *Biblical Approaches to Pastoral Counseling* (Westminster Press, 1981), pp. 47–95. But we do not concur with Capps's use of the Kübler-Ross stages as a pattern for understanding grief.

28. Bowlby, *The Making and Breaking of Affectional Bonds*, p. 64.

29. Lindemann, *Beyond Grief*, p. 61.

30. Tappert, ed., *Luther: Letters of Spiritual Counsel*, p. 68.

31. Ibid., p. 67.

32. Lewis, *A Grief Observed*, p. 47.

33. Ibid., p. 49.

34. William Butler Yeats, "A Deep-Sworn Vow," *Collected Poems* (Macmillan Co., 1956), p. 152.

35. Our argument that at a deep emotional level there is no such thing as divorce is reflected in Robert Farrar Capon's books, *Bed and Board* (William Morrow & Co., 1965) and *A Second Day* (William Morrow & Co., 1980). In both books Capon refers to divorce as a metaphysical impossibility. *Bed and Board* was written when Capon was apparently happily married and presumably had never actively contemplated a divorce. *A Second Day*, on the other hand, is a reflection on divorce and remarriage. In this latter book Capon reaffirms the argument that divorce is a metaphysical impossibility, that in fact one does not have an *ex*-wife, but rather a wife with whom one is no longer living and with whom one has entered into a new contractual arrangement. Thus there may be, at law, such a thing as divorce, but theologically or metaphysically there is not; the "one flesh" assertion is to be taken with utter seriousness. From a psychological perspective there is also no such thing as divorce, even though the loss one undergoes in a legal divorce is a real loss.

36. Arthur John Gossip, "But When Life Tumbles In, What Then?" in Andrew W. Blackwood, *The Protestant Pulpit* (Abing-

don-Cokesbury Press, 1947), pp. 198ff. Gossip's reference to the River Eunoë is a call to warm reminiscence which, as we shall see in the next chapter, is an important aspect of grieving with which ministers can help greatly. Gossip's sermon, frequently reprinted, is anthologized by Blackwood as a master sermon. Copies of it are frequently given by pastors to grieving persons, and it is sometimes thought of as a major "gem" about grief. But the careful reader will notice that the attitude Gossip espouses in this sermon is in its fundamentals a Stoic attitude misperceived as a Christian one. Gossip admonishes himself and his hearers to show no feelings, or as few as possible, and implies that having pain or anger at all bespeaks a lack of faith on the part of a grief-stricken person. Stoicism is a major rival to Christian faith in our day, though seldom identified for what it is. It is in fact often identified as a Christian attitude rather than a pagan philosophy. Some cultures in today's world, including our own, place a very high value on keeping one's feelings out of conscious awareness or at least out of the notice of others. Such an attitude receives no support from biblical Christianity.

37. Norman L. Paul and George H. Grosser, "Operational Mourning and Its Role in Conjoint Family Therapy," *Community Mental Health Journal*, Vol. 1 (Winter 1965). In a similar way, Charles Gerkin has linked bereavement and patterns of family interaction in *Crisis Experience in Modern Life* (Abingdon Press, 1979), pp. 110–161.

38. John Calvin, *Commentary on the Epistles of Paul the Apostle to the Philippians, Colossians, and Thessalonians* (Wm. B. Eerdmans Publishing Co., 1948), pp. 279–280.

39. Cf. the following commentaries: Leon Morris, *The Epistles of Paul to the Thessalonians* (Wm. B. Eerdmans Publishing Co., 1957), p. 67, and *The First and Second Epistles to the Thessalonians* (Wm. B. Eerdmans Publishing Co., 1959), p. 95; William Neil, *Saint Paul's Epistles to the Thessalonians* (London: SCM Press, 1957), p. 95; D. E. H. Whitely, *Thessalonians in the Revised Standard Version* (London: Oxford University Press, 1969), p. 66.

40. Walter Brueggeman, "Covenanting as Human Vocation," *Interpretation*, Vol. 23 (1979).

41. Norman Paul, "The Use of Empathy in the Resolution of Grief," *Perspectives in Biology and Medicine*, Autumn 1967, pp. 153–169. "The ability of the therapist to empathize with grief and other painful states seems related to his capacity for reflective review of feelings generated by comparable situations in his own life." (P. 164).

42. Caine, *Widow*, p. 109.

43. Lewis, *A Grief Observed*, p. 23.

44. Simone de Beauvoir, *A Very Easy Death* (Warner Paperback Library, 1973), p. 106. This book is a moving account of the death of de Beauvoir's mother.

45. Joyce A. Phipps, "What Really Happens When Your Husband Dies?" *Christian Century*, Vol. 90 (Feb. 21, 1973), pp. 230–232.

46. Herbert Anderson, "The Impact of the Death of a Parent on Middle-Aged Children," *Pastoral Psychology*, Vol. 28 (Spring 1980).

47. Daniel J. Simundson, *Faith Under Fire* (Augsburg Publishing House, 1980).

48. Lewis, *A Grief Observed*, p. 54.

49. Capon, *Bed and Board*. Cf. note 35.

50. Geoffrey Rowell, *The Liturgy of Christian Burial* (London: S.P.C.K., 1977); Paul Irion, *The Funeral and the Mourners* (Abingdon Press, 1954); John P. Meier, "Catholic Funerals in the Light of Scripture," *Worship*, Vol. 48, No. 4, pp. 206–216; Paul Waitman Hoon, "Theology, Death, and the Funeral Liturgy," *Union Seminary Quarterly Review*, Vol. 31, No. 3 (Spring 1976), pp. 169–181.

51. Joseph Matthews, "The Time My Father Died," *Motive*, Jan. 1964.

52. Ibid.

53. Kenneth R. Mitchell and Herbert Anderson, "You Must Leave Before You Can Cleave: A Family Systems Approach to Premarital Work," *Pastoral Psychology*, Vol. 30 (Winter 1981).

54. Through their administrative structures and through educational programs, local congregations are often helpful to members who are undergoing losses of various kinds. The Board of Deacons of Westminster United Presbyterian Church, Dubuque, Iowa, produced a valuable manual used by the pastor, the board itself, and members of the congregation at times of loss. Other congregations have regular adult education programs in this area. Still others sponsor groups such as THEOS (They Help Each Other Survive), which is designed to provide an opportunity for widows and widowers to share grieving processes with each other.

55. William Lynch, *Images of Hope* (New American Library of World Literature, 1965).

56. The widely varying translations into various contemporary languages of this beatitude—as of much of the biblical text—are evidence of the way in which theological presuppositions are

built into translating. There can be little doubt that the New
Testament Greek phrase *hoi penthountes* refers to an active,
emotion-laden process of weeping. Such a construction, the
present active participle of a verb that denotes active pain and
sorrow, is also found in a contemporary Russian version of the
Bible, in which the word *plachushchie* is both morphologically and
etymologically the exact equivalent of the Greek. Other translations convey a different meaning. The French *les affligés* and the
English of the NEB ("the sorrowful") convey a quite different
sense. There are also contemporary commentators who assume
without arguing their case that what the "mourners" mourn is
their sins. At least in the Greek text there is no evidence for this
assumption. What the New Testament original refers to, so far as
we can see, is quite close to the raw expression of emotion which
we have insisted is a necessary component of grieving.

57. Dietrich Bonhoeffer, *The Cost of Discipleship* (Macmillan Co.,
1958), p. 92.

58. Ibid., p. 93.

59. We have said little throughout this book about the cost of
helping. Pastoral theology, in our opinion, has in fact slighted the
personal characteristics of the pastor, the cost to the pastor of
extending help, and most related topics. But the person of the
helper is a primary question that needs careful understanding.
How much pain can one person bear? What is the cost to any
helper, ordained pastor or committed layperson, of listening on
an hours-long, day-in-day-out basis to those whose sorrow is
overwhelming them? We are aware that, as pastors ourselves, we
have a tendency to listen with reduced sympathy to our own
families when we have been in the presence of "real" suffering.
We are tempted to say to our own loved ones, "You don't know
how lucky you are"; and sometimes that is what we do say. We
raise this question here to remind ourselves and our readers that
the ability to care really does depend upon our understanding
that it is ultimately the suffering Lord who takes upon himself
these burdens, as well as the burdens of parishioners.

60. Paul Tillich, *Systematic Theology*, Vol. II: *Existence and the
Christ* (University of Chicago Press, 1957), p. 70.

61. Walter Brueggemann, "The Formfulness of Grief," *Interpretation*, Vol. 31 (1977), pp. 263–275.

62. Dorothee Soelle, *Suffering* (Fortress Press, 1975), p. 32.